FUNDAMENTALS OF AGRICULTURAL ECONOMICS

FUNDAMENTALS OF AGRICULTURAL ECONOMICS

(With Perspectives from Indian Agriculture)

Chandrahas H. Shah

KALPAZ

Fundamentals of Agricultural Economics

ISBN: 978-81-7835-944-1

Published in 2013 in India by
Kalpaz Publications
C-30, Satyawati Nagar,
Delhi-110052
E-mail: kalpaz@hotmail.com
Phone : 9212729499

Lasser Type Setting by: Rudra Computer Graphics, Delhi
Printed at : G. Print Process.Delhi

Dedicated

With Love and Gratitude
to the
Revered Founder Chancellor
Sri Sathya Sai
Institute of Higher Learning
Sri Sathya Sai Baba

Contents

Gratitude

It was His grace that gave an opportunity to me to undertake this study. I penned down the words but they came from Him. The problems and solutions suggested in this study are His and credit for them belongs to Him. If there are still some shortcomings which a sharp eye can detect, the discredit for them goes to me. I take this opportunity to heartily thank Bhagavan Sri Sathya Sai Baba, Revered Founder Chancellor, Sri Sathya Sai Institute of Higher Learning, Prasanthe Nilayam, Chandrahas H. Shah, Andhra Pradesh. He prompted and guided the study at all stages.

Foreword

Agricultural production is space-based because land, the major input is itself space-based. In contrast, production in non-agricultural sectors is basically time-based. Increased production in industries is possible by compressing time taken for production processes. Increased production in agriculture is obtained by compressing space over which production is based in usual parlance referred to as intensive cultivation. Water is yet another input for agricultural production, and major source of water is rainfall. Thus, weather as a whole impacts farm production very significantly. If rainwater is stored either underground in tanks or behind high dames, stored water make irrigation possible. Irrigation helps reduce exclusive dependence on rain. These basic characters of agriculture and non-agricultural production determine development of production systems for agriculture and non-agricultural sectors somewhat differently. Ignoring these differences leads to problems in designing effective strategies intended to modernise agricultural production system in developing nations.

Moreover, agricultural production system is predominantly a micro-system. In irrigation modernisation is developed on micro irrigation. Micro finance too has fairly quickly made good progress. However, the marketing system continues to be traditional and largely conducive to benefiting the non-agricultural sectors. Thus, while micro marketing is needed, the model followed is different and starkly out of line.

The present study traces in detail how agriculture developed in the past, and what developments are likely to follow under the present system. This gives us some clues with regard to what policy initiatives are required for the future development. The urban and rural societies are fairly strongly linked through agriculture because it provides the basic food and raw materials for urban economic development. A strong and sustained development of the agricultural sector is obviously the foundation for overall economic development of the economy.

For, India and more generally almost all developing economies, a rapid and sustained growth of agriculture is vastly more important because an overwhelming part of the population not only depends on agriculture but is also abysmally poor. The study points out with clear understanding that the intermediate stage of modernising agriculture to help modernised urban economy is painful. The need for a humane solution is thus urgently called for. The study is therefore focused to identify concepts and suggested solution based on human-values. This values-based economic development draws heavily on the ideas given by Sri Sathya Sai in early 1980's. Sri Sathya Sai Institute of Higher Learning has experimented with values-based education in different branches of education, on which the author draws significantly.

Last but not the least; the study is most welcome as it is appropriately timed to coincide with the 30th year of the Institute.

Prof. Vishwanath Pandit
Vice-Chancellor (2008-2010)
Sri Sathya Sai Institute of Higher Learning
(Deemed to be University)
Prasanthi Nilayam - 515134
Anantapur (District)
Andhra Pradesh, India

Preface

The author had experience of teaching and research in the subject for a period of nearly three decades. During this period the author was engaged in unraveling the cross inter-connections among the economic trends and the human elements which are essential for understanding the problem and behaviour of the actors that play a vital role in the economic operations.

We understand the complexities through the beliefs that we carry for decades if not centuries. The beliefs change but the essence remains unchanged. Such beliefs add to the complexities of the perceived human behaviour.

Over a period of fifty years after two World Wars and period between them is the witness to the changes in the human behaviour at all levels. We have to go back into the period of human history when agriculture took a slow start. And the period of start of agriculture was a move away from 'fight or fright'. Living on killing of animals and gathering fruits and grains was the main or only source of livelihood. When grains entered the livelihood, land, labour and water (rain or river or underground) were the main inputs and the product like grain was the main output. The economic and social organisation of the society was around it. When the mean of exchange changed the grain became a value based medium of savings, instead of society based on mutual help and compassion and greed entered the social organization. This greed element influenced not only producers but also those who engaged in business of exchange called trade.

Exchange helped progress. The development of production was helped as the implements of processing were invented. Grinding mill helped wheat and other cereals. Rice was invented earlier, for boiling was done with the help of fire. Rolling stone and rolling pins helped further to have the cooked products of cereals. Savings gave way to taste for cooked food could not be stored for long period of time and hence could not be saved in the final form.

The main frame of theory was based on this process of development. Theory of rent by Ricardo and the theory of basic goods by Sraffa much later are two major examples. Then came the urban development. Many recent economic problems we face can be traced to the urbanisation and attending problem of greed and commercialisation. As greed increased so increased commerce and so declined compassion and performance of the society in terms of human quality. If we trace back we shall come to the conclusion that the organisation will have to be revamped with human values in the center. In this monograph we try to raise the issue and point to the possible solution.

Prof G. Bhalchandran
Dean, Faculty of Humanities and Economics
Sri Sathya Sai Institute of Higher Learnings
Prasanthi Nilayam

Acknowledgements

Divinity guides, humans play the role. Prof Vishwanath Pandit encouraged this study like. He was the then Vice-Chancellor. I came in his contact when he was the Head of the Department of Economics before he assumed the office of the Vice-Chancellor at the Sri Sathya Sai Institute of Higher Learning. He had contributed a Foreword to an earlier study relating to the problems of drought prone areas in India. Prof. G. Bhalchandran and Prof. K.L.N. Reddy were associated with me for study. I participated in teaching as a visiting faculty at the Sri Sathya Sai Institute. I benefited from them through interactions with other members of the department.

The study of the nature presented here is product of work of years. Prof Dantwala, Head, Department of Economics, University of Bombay (now Mumbai) and also Director of the Department of Economics who was associated since the inception of the Agricultural Economics Section, was my teacher and later a colleague. The present study owes to him the valuable insights provided by continued interactions and even joint works with him. Colleagues in the department made their contributions to my understanding of the subject. Over the years the professional friends made their contributions in the development of my thinking and understanding of the vast and deep contents of the subject like agricultural economics. It is difficult to name them all. But I would be missing in my duty if I do not mention V.M. Rao who willingly gave his feedback for my works during my visiting faculty position in the Sri Sathya Sai Institute of Higher Learning. My association with him stretches to our days together in University of Bombay.

I am thankful to my grandson, Dr. Shashank Shah, Post-Doctoral Fellow, Faculty of Management and Commerce, Sri Sathya Sai Institute of Higher Learning, Prashanti Nilayam, for coordinating the publication of this work. An accomplished researcher in the area of corporate Governance, Stakeholders Management and Values-based Business, he assisted with his meticulous proof reading and also suggested the design for the cover page. Mr. Radha Preetam, Student of the M.A.(Economics) programme at the institute executed the cover page design as suggested by Dr Shashank Shah, aesthetically.My appreciation is also due to Kalpaz Publications, Delhi for bringing out this work in a professional form.

CHANDRAHAS H. SHAH

1

Some Basic Characteristics

Basic its characteristics of production processes of any sector mould the entire sector. Agriculture is not an industry because of its basic characteristics. Efforts to mould agriculture into industry have yet not yielded results. Agriculture remains till now basically a sector of individual producer. The major inputs like land and water are nature's gifts. Efforts have been made and still continue for changing the production processes to increase the inputs that are man-made and thus give it a character of the industry sector. There has been limited success. Industries have basically continuous production. In agriculture, weather plays a major role and that makes it discontinuous from season to season.

Due to the above stated difference in the basic characteristics of agriculture and industries, we examine these characteristics and issues arising from them. Agriculture is one of the oldest occupations. It began with hunting and gathering. Then it transited to settled cultivation. At no stage did it resemble the industry. The land, water and human labour together with minimum of capital like seeds are the basic inputs. The proportion varied mainly because of natural supply of water like rainfall. Rivers were another source of water. When irrigation entered the skill of growing crops, the production attained a relatively comparable level of production from one year to the next. Till then crop production varied from year to year and so also the levels of inputs. Nor did the levels of inputs varied in proportion of output.

Fields have uneven land, and water received from uneven rainfall. There is uneven relation if any, between inputs and output. Over a period of time – centuries - more rapidly during the recent decades – helped by irrigation, fertilizers and pesticides aided by irrigation has brought agriculture close to a status of industries sector. Year 2009 monsoon still reminds us of the days of the years gone by, the days of famine which we now experience in Northern India and parts of Western India.

We bring in two semi-inputs to make agriculture look like an industry. They are storage and processing. Demand for food is continuous, it would not vary from day to day. The uneven output of crops over years in the past necessitated storage like PATARA a traditional storage device. (District Gazetteer-Anantpur District). It needs to be remembered that PATARA were in use for local purposes. The inter-war period made PATARA look like things of the past and extinct. Then the storage was in use for strictly local purposes and mainly for the family. But with the development of markets to dispose of the marketable surplus through the market agencies like *Pucca and Kachha Adatias* dalals, brokers and finally futures markets through various channels, storage became a part of marketing activities. The harvest started to flow in the market even within the year of production. Instead of local storage, for consumption to be smooth during the year has now been for financial transactions. Hypothecation made possible to have loans from financial institutions like banks. What was sold during the harvest season some times returned to the local area if the production turned out to be insufficient or was required for consumption during the off season. Especially labour class would need to buy grains for their consumption needs. When there is no work for agriculture during the off season, employment ebbs and so also the wages. Farmers take up work for investment like digging wells or storage devices. So also repair and maintenance of house, cattle-shed and more importantly land improvement like land levelling, gully plugging, etc. All these works depend on financial position of farmers and availability of labour at going wage rate.

There are two points that need attention. Labour needs work, but also needs sustenance while on work. Those who do not earn enough during lean season and had little to store by; buy their needs from the market resulting into flow of grain in the reverse direction.

Farming involves by and large physical labour. Capital substituting land or labour to a major extent is less likely for agriculture practiced in India and other developing nations and especially women folk have a relatively larger share in it. Besides kitchen and cooking work, cleaning and washing women participate in farming during cultivation season as a helper for work relating to irrigation, weeding, harvesting, bundling of straw and thrashing and often winnowing etc. Summer season is mostly devoted to social events in the family or community. Much of the processing work like removing the husk from paddy and making wheat ready for storage so that it does not deteriorate in quality has to be done after the harvest comes home. This is changing and Mahnis are taking over some of the processes. But bulk of the labour is still engaged in the post harvest processes. Among farming families there is a proverb that, "there are twelve months in a year but there are thirteen months of work." This brings out the feelings of farmers, their family members and workers employed on salary. Yet we have evidence that leads many to conclude that in farming there is distinct evidence of unemployment. We shall deal with this problem of apparent unemployment and implied over-employment. But at this point we may observe that unlike industrial employment and unemployment, there is lack of clarity about measure of agricultural employment and unemployment.

A similar lack of clarity exists and is faced regarding the valuation of the produce and its cost. The farmer is both a consumer and a producer of the harvest on his farm. As such his business consists of a buyer and a seller and the price of his produce has two levels of valuation. As a buyer he would value his harvest at harvest price, the price at which he would sell his harvest.

In the traditional farming, most of the time farmers would be sellers and the pressure on sale may require him to dispose of most of the surplus he has soon after the harvest. This applies to most if not all farmers. Small farmers with tiny holdings have to sell the entire production soon after the harvest is ready. The result is inevitable. The price he gets is lower than price he pays later when he runs short of supplies with him. More traditional an economy, greater would be the gap between the two prices and greater is the gap between the harvest prices and off season prices. This is some time interpreted as the gap representing exploitation by the trading community. This is partially true. It is true that the situation created by the natural situation caused by weather pattern and partly by the consumption pattern. If the pattern for storage can be modified, part of the sharpness of weather effect on prices can be smoothened.

This has not happened for two reasons. If loans were easily available when needed, then the holding capacity of farmers can be increased and the earning power too can be increased. In the traditional societies, there were traditional methods of storage which not only helped overcome the stress of drought and famine conditions but also helped smoothen the inter-season gap in prices.

Two more points need to be added. As an economic decision-maker, the farmer considered flush of revenue earned at the harvest time as income for purchases and thus speedily denuded the purchasing power. And some time, over-spent the resources beyond his capacity. Where he should have budget that would help the spending required during the off season, in absence of such budgeting the matching of expenditure and earning becomes a gamble. Gamble is all the more so if we consider the period beyond the calendar year. For illustration, what seems to be a surplus at the beginning could result into a negative balance towards the end and thus upset the financial calculations. Those endowed with skill of financial calculation will be the winner in this game. Thus, besides the uncertainty of weather, low skill of calculation can also add imperfection in decision-making.

One point still remains for us to complete our discussion at this stage. The very fact that communication between rural areas and urban centers is full of obstacles. The roads are not linked and transport is slow and time consuming especially for those who live in remote areas. Inconvenient transport adds to the cost and time for transport. This may be taken further advantage of by intermediaries for their own profits.

Further, the market is not well organized. The products need better standardization and better agency to overcome disputes. We need at an advance stage futures markets to cover risks for farmers and intermediaries. All these need to be provided on top of separate credit agencies. Where credit and marketing are combined, the scales are tipped in favour of intermediaries. Research works show that the price received by farmers is negatively related to the distance from the market. This has been observed in the case of groundnut in Saurashtra. (Jasadanwala) and in regard to cotton in Maharashtra (Dantwala – Marketing of Raw Cotton in India). The former suggests costs scale up with distance and the latter suggests the scaling up is smooth. Both are partial observations. The observations were based on simple analysis. But both go to suggest that there is no direct evidence of imperfect or perfect competition at both ends. We have no evidence to compare the results of price behaviour in perfect market with that in imperfect market. Evidence available covers up imperfection, if any.

Food and non-food crops are mainly non-perishable (over short periods like one season or one year and especially food crops are for farm family. For farm family they are consumable as well as marketable crops. We observed so far that this character creates a market level gap in prices. The gap is further affected by the market characteristics discussed earlier. It is this gap in prices over the season which is indicative of producer-consumer characteristic gap. Greater the size of the gap, greater the characteristic of agriculture being traditional. It also gets complicated by characteristics of the market.

Thus, the basic characteristics are mainly three. The major inputs are land and water together with human labour. Capital so far has a smaller role to play. Weather affects output and variations could be vide from one year to next. Third characteristic is that the product is for consumption and partially for market. The storage has been split between the farmer family and market. Farmers are dragged between the two. What is marketed is bought back later in the year. This may be due to miscalculation of needs for the consumption.

2

Fundamentals of Indian Agriculture

Is agriculture fundamentally for subsistence and/or for development? This question was asked by economists in the olden times, some 250 years ago by Physiocrats in France. Malthus's main thesis too supported the fundamental characteristic of agriculture. Before Ricardo and Marshal, the Phisyocrats raised this question and answered too. Unless agriculture provides and continues to provide food to those engaged in non-agricultural activities in addition to providing food for those engaged in agriculture, the non-agricultural activities would not be sustained and definitely would not expand. Agricultural production would not expand once the limit to the expansion of land under cultivation is reached. The only alternative would be increased productivity of land. Since the land supply is limited, the prospect for extensive cultivation by adding acreage to cultivated area is less likely. Increasing land productivity would require two conditions to be fulfilled. The technology of production has to change and the inputs substituting land have to expand. And this process has to continue in time for the economy as a whole to expand. The crux here is the moving of labour out of agriculture so that larger and larger proportion of working population is engaged in production of non-agricultural products and services. The farming community has to expand production to feed the expanding labour force outside agriculture In developing economies like India the problem is that a huge proportion of the working force engaged in agriculture is already high and in most cases it is declining at a slow pace.

Wage goods theory propounded by some economists implies the same proposition. Ricardo through his theory of diminishing marginal product came to the similar conclusion. The absence of technological change in the case of Ricardo's scenario would lead to grinding down of the process of expansion of crop production. Even while crop production is expanding by adding more labour to existing land under cultivation, the diminishing marginal product proposition would imply reducing per worker addition to production. The wages and hence income levels would tend to decline.

In recent literature once again we have the echo of the same question and we come across the same or similar answer. Prof. T.W. Schultz in his seminal work on agricultural development (Transforming Traditional Agriculture) reminded us of the zero marginal productivity of labour in agriculture in traditional economies where the technological change is expected to be low or absent.

Preponderance of workers engaged in agriculture in the developing economies as against their miniscule share in the total GDP, this unalterable situation facing developing economies gave rise to the repeated proposition of agriculture being the Achilles' heel in the less developed economies.

Two major issues have emerged allied to the main question of agriculture being fundamental to economic development. The most widely discussed and easily accepted outgrowth is that of widespread un- or under- employment in developing economies, including India. And further, it is suggested that the stock of unutilized or underutilized labour can be turned into the source of growth. Lewis, the major proponent of this theory, has been supported by many economists from the developing economies. With exposition to the institutions like practice of share rent in agriculture, the economists from developing economies have provided the support for the theory of surplus labour in the economy, mainly in the agriculture.

Agricultural fundamentalism is propagated even in developed economy; there the argument of absence of technological change is replaced by sociological and political considerations. The end result, however, is only apparently different. Both in developing and developed economies the agricultural policies are colored by the basic contention implied in agricultural fundamentalism. The programmes of price support, subsidies in various forms and investment in agriculture draw their sustenance from the argument underlying the agricultural fundamentalism

In India, the conditions differed during the British rule and after independence. The alien rulers were guided in policy formation by the economic interests of the home country. The basic consideration was availability of food and raw materials supplied by agriculture in the colonial country at low or below market prices. We shall see that during the British period, agricultural progress was confined to market or cash crops and the taxation policy was inimical to the interests of the farming community. Heavy tax burden (of land revenue in British ruled states especially) constrained the saving capacity and thus restricted the investment and consequently the desired growth of agriculture. The yields per hectare (or acre) were largely stagnant or even declining, (Dantwala). Alongside, however, in select crops the quality of output was improving. This is illustrated by Basmati rice. Basmati replaced in some instances the short duration paddy crop. While population was stagnant or marginally expanding during the pre-independence period sluggish agricultural production made little impact on consumption levels.

India, however, shared with other nations, world over, the mortal blow of depression of thirties. Prices of all products nose-dived. Agricultural prices too declined. While for other industries the painful option of closing down and thus limiting the losses was open, for agriculture by its very nature the option of closing down or down-sizing was unavailable. For the period, the theme of agricultural fundamentalism went into the background. But incomes of farming community including farm labour fell precipitously. Labour that lost employment in non-agricultural sectors returned to rural areas. Their return added to the burden already unbearable. The economy as a whole was in doldrums. The key to economic ailment was in micro-economic behaviour. Agriculture as such was short-shrifted. India could not escape this world-wide phenomenon. The inflexible land tax made the burden back-breaking.

Indian agriculture not only inherited the heavy financial burden of the inadvisable economic policy of alien rulers, but also had underlying special geographic features that were not attended to, to help to return to normalcy. Drought-prone areas were left behind. But in the meanwhile, World War II intervened. The story of war economy has a different tale to tell.

Before we understand the underlying principles that explain the rise and decline of the phenomenon of surplus labour observed and efforts made by economists to explain it over a long period of time, we shall look into the basic characteristics of agriculture in India.

India has specific physical characteristics that set India apart from many less developed economies. They mould of the organization of institutions that affect the organization of production in agriculture. Two major characteristics may be noted first. They are mainly physical or geographical in nature.

In the first place, India has a monsoon season. Rainfall in most part of the country is received during the four months of the season in a year. Within the season in most places, 60 to 80 per cent of precipitation is concentrated in 60 days or less. Even during this core season the rainfall is not uniformly distributed. Forecasting of the rain useful for cultivation of land and planting of seeds is highly difficult. The pattern does not repeat from one year to the next. Harvesting season is equally unpredictable. In most cases, harvesting is concentrated within a short period of time. This is seen mostly in the case of minor cereals. They are grown mostly in drought-prone regions. On the other hand, cotton has relatively much longer harvest time. Hence cotton is sometimes known as a two-season crop.

Not only is the rainfall within a given year less predictable but also its distribution from one year to the next is less predictable. There are regions in India in which flood is an annual feature and there are regions in which the drought is endemic[1]. These regions are not marginal. They account for a significant part of the total area. It is this lack of predictability of season that has given the epitome of 'a gamble in rain' to agriculture in India[2].

This specific character of agriculture especially in India leads to inevitable consequences. I shall deal with them in detail later. Here I indicate the broad implications. The major implication relates to employment in agriculture. We are used to viewing continuous or uninterrupted work schedule over the work year in occupations other than agriculture especially in secondary and tertiary sectors. The rural services and handicrafts and industries processing agricultural output are an exception to the secondary sector in general. They have seasonal pattern of work resembling that to agriculture in some measure. But the peaks and troughs of non-agricultural rural occupations are less severe than that of agriculture. In agriculture at the peak, hours of work to be put in may be much beyond the 8-hour work day, and the work week may run into week-ends. There may thus be long stretches of continuous work and correspondingly there may be light work or even no work during other parts of the year. The absence of work during some part of the year may give an impression of near unemployment situation. Measuring unemployment in agriculture is tricky and measures evolved are in some ways arbitrary. The fact that a worker otherwise engaged in helping the family if asked whether he or she will be available for work[3] may give an answer which would be vague in character. In the mind of the person answering the question there may be no clear idea regarding the wage attached to the additional work. It is not implied that there is always full employment for the people working in agriculture in various regions with varying weather conditions. But a severe caution needs to be exercised.

Other major features pertain to distribution of land, production pattern and marketing and allied credit operations. We refer to the period largely before the initiation of the planning and of late of ushering in of Green Revolution.

Indian agriculture survived the step-motherly treatment given by the alien rulers till 1947. Agriculture adjusted from time to time to the demands of time. Irrigation of various forms helped increase the production capacity. Dug wells were known for long time. Since 1930's mechanization of water lifting devices like oil-engines with pump substituting bullock-driven traditional leather bags (locally called KOS) as water lifting devices or like them, including even DHEKADI (crow bar like device) and Persian wheels (locally called RNET) was mainly at the initiative of the individual producers. In some parts the increased capacity for irrigation by introduction of oil engines and electric motors and pumps led to the development of market of irrigation water as observed in some parts of India. In Gujarat, simple mechanization of irrigation system was aided in part by flow of funds from family members migrating to parts of Africa.

Introduction of groundnut in Saurashtra and sugar cane in UP and then in Maharashtra on cooperative basis are illustrations of local initiative for growth and development. Expansion of area under cotton was partly in response to growing textile industry within the country and demand for cotton abroad especially in United Kingdom. The alien rulers took initiative mainly to sustain economic progress of home country and support there industrial expansion. When USA passed through the civil war era, the international trade of cotton especially to United Kingdom was disrupted. This disruption provided fillip to cotton production in India. With expansion of irrigation in Punjab before partition of the country, encouraged growing of long staple cotton for which the market was expanding. These developments illustrate robustness of agriculture regarding change and growth.

Despite these examples of robustness of agriculture regarding change and adjustment to changes we cannot claim that agriculture was modernized. Till 1941, population growth was modest. Both birth and death rates were high making the survival rate low. But traditionally, the country had relatively high population density. Absence of industrial growth of large magnitude, made agriculture the main stay for population to eke out a living. The result was inevitably one of shrinking size of average farm.

The size of land holding varied, it was minuscule in relatively fertile area with relatively assured rainfall. Parts of eastern and northern region, and part of southern region had relatively small holdings. Where size of holding was comparatively larger, the low and uncertain rainfall and low irrigation potential made living precarious. Both these conditions made agriculture mainly a family farming. Absence of infrastructure facilities also constrained market involvement of agriculture. Crops were primarily grown for self- or family-consumption. For years the marketed surplus hovered around 20 per cent of total food gain production. When production is primarily for self- consumption it is inevitable that the crops grown varied according to the local preferences. We had regions that grew mainly the millets and other regions where rice dominated. Some areas grew wheat.

The market operations covered mostly the trickle that flowed mainly to urban areas in small driblets. The limited size of crop entering the market from distances made marketing a cost-heavy operation. The infrastructure facilities favoured mainly the movement of goods from cities in the hinterland to ports for exports. Poor infrastructure facilities in rural area further added to the cost of moving crops. The marketing margins thus tended to be wider compared to that in the developed countries. This happened despite the developed future markets in cotton and wheat. Outlying areas and distant villages which had relatively greater share of their production used for self-consumption, suffered a disadvantage in the price received at the market for their trickle reaching the market.

Production of crops requires finance. The crop growing starts with land cultivation. Planting of seeds takes place soon after the monsoon rains arrive. Harvest is ready after 90 days in the case of millets and 160 to 180 days in the case of rice.

Cotton is nearly two-season crop, wheat was grown as single crop during the winter season. The crop schedule thus spread over months. During that period the family has to maintain itself. The lucky few who were in a position to carry over enough supply from the previous year, needed limited credit if any. Others had to borrow for buying seeds year after year for they had not enough income that would permit saving. The need for credit was met traditionally by borrowing from relatives who had surplus and traders and money lenders. Banking institutions came into existence around the World War I. Banks advanced loans mainly to commerce sector on hypothecation basis. Their share in loans to agriculture was insignificant. Cooperative societies came in to existence around the same time. They engaged in loans to farmers for production purposes. Need for purchasing grain for self consumption during the production season was not recognized as productive use then. The restrictive practices of cooperatives, insufficient funds and bad debts made cooperatives too an unimportant source of borrowing by farmers. The precarious financial conditions led to usurious loan practices by private agencies. The private lenders however carried the major part of the risk involved in unpredictable harvest. The economic depression during 1930s made agriculture an uneconomic enterprise. Debts mounted. Additionally the tax on land, known as land revenue, an unbearable burden. Land revenue in Ryotwari areas governed by British rulers was fixed during relatively better times. When the times changed and condition worsened the borrowing put heavy financial burden on peasants resulting in many cases defaulting and subsequent usurping of lands by the state for collecting revenue dues. The local money lenders were harsher in their dealings with farmers. Areas not directly governed by alien rulers were under domination of land lords or Zamindars. They too were not kind or humane. They followed Britishers in pursuing exploitation policies.

World wars are in themselves not welcome. They involve huge losses of life and property. However, the World War II came as a much needed financial relief for farmers especially in

India. With improved financial position mainly due to runaway inflation during war time, many farmers could redeem their debts. Investment too increased which helped growing more non-food crops despite legal restrictions imposed by the administration as a part of war efforts. On the whole farmers had limited benefits from the rising prices since the price rise was curbed by food grain rationing on one hand, and restriction on growing non-food crops on the other. Compulsory levy of food grains added further restriction to motivation for expanding food grains production.

Technological improvement needs a research base. During the alien rule only a small beginning was made. Agricultural departments were set up in some provinces towards the end of 19th century. Between the 1890s and 1930s some improved varieties were available. Most of them brought in improved quality. As already mentioned for rice for instance improved Basmati varieties reached the market in increased quantity. We have mentioned about the long staple cotton varieties introduced in the Punjab. Sugar was an exception. Better variety helped increase yield per acre. The new variety of sugar cane was brought from Hawaii. It had higher sugar (sucrose) content too. Beside the efforts regarding crop production, efforts were made to improve quality of animals to help better performance for cultivation and improve the fat content of milk. This related to cows. Royal Commission on Agriculture (1930) recommended setting up of Institutions at the Central level for research work in agriculture. Indian Council of Agricultural Research was set up pursuing the Royal Commission recommendation.

While progress was seen, most of it pertained to crops for market and pertained to quality improvement. Organised efforts thus pertained less to the needs of the producer who would have preferred to produce more for self consumption. The latter would have required research relating to local varieties. Some efforts like making compost and using it for manure was recommended but farmers did not accept it enthusiastically. Compost required water during summer time when water was scarce or unavailable. Towards the end of 1930s the department tried to introduce groundnut meal as a supplement to cow dung manure. These sporadic efforts did not add up to massive efforts needed for increased production.

All told, the result was unable to make impact on land productivity till the end of 1930s. Subsequent increase in population and rising income along with it during the initial years of War followed by independence led to the food scarcity which nearly resulted into supply crisis till Green Revolution made real head way in 1970s. We had local varieties in place. They were evolved over centuries with quality to fight the local pests and diseases. That helped them survive till present time. The non-food crops such as cotton, tobacco, oilseeds gained ground in a significant way in some regions. That helped improve cash inflows. All these efforts did not help to have sizeable growth of agriculture till the planning was initiated in 1950s after independence of the nation.

Plans initiated massive investment in agriculture in the public sector. Especially irrigation got the boost. The evaluation of the impact of planning and subsequent Green Revolution two decades later will be taken up in the subsequent chapters.

Before I end, I would touch upon the structure of agriculture, especially regarding the land holding, ownership, tenancy and landlessness. The detailed study of the structure will require one separate chapter. Here I would like to deal with the features of the structure inherited at the time of independence. I have mentioned that the holdings were small and the size was declining as the population growth continued unabated after independence.

Indian agriculture was considered as traditional and often described as a way of living rather than an economic activity. The implied contention was that the producers would not respond to economic signals like prices and production will be aimed at self-consumption. It was also contended that the structure of agriculture we inherited was archaic and discouraged expansion through right type of investment. I have mentioned that despite this sporadic development like use of oil engines, etc. did occur but its impact was limited to certain regions. The two major characteristics of structure of land holding pointed out by observers were viz. the strong hold of Zamindari and extensive prevalence of rent in kind and also wages in kind. It is contended that both led to usurious practice that impacted adversely the efficient use of resources.

Zamindars had land holdings of varying sizes and they wielded variety of powers. Where Zamindari was a relic of the past and the Zamindars enjoyed the administrative and military powers. Some of them had under their control land of the size of a district. Elsewhere where the states were mere principalities, Zamindars owned land almost equal to big holders. The economic incentive was subsidiary for them. As already mentioned, they indulged, following the British Government, in extracting most from the Raiyat (meaning subject) or cultivators. The collection of dues was in many cases in kind. The cultivators in turn would engage labour on wages in kind. Wages in kind were in terms of share or in terms of piece or time rate. The practise of paying wages in kind or piece wages prevailed for the labour engaged for harvesting of crops with operations including winnowing, etc.

The web of relationship among the landlords and occupants and types of labour was complex. The upshot of these relationships was dilution or suppression of operation of economic forces. In this sense, the farming practised at the time of independence was largely traditional and hence a way of life. As we shall see subsequently, the Five Year Plans concentrated initially on reforming the land structure along with investment in the public sector and various other measures relating to prices, credit and scientific advancement through research and education and extension.

We now move to taking the true measure of the traditional phase of Indian agriculture so that we can fathom the challenges facing the nation when the nation achieved independence. Once the job is well defined for the country, we will be able to analyze the measure adopted and the problems now faced for the better future in the 21st century and beyond.

Thus, at the time of initiation of planning the two major steps that were given priority were firstly public sector investment in irrigation and manufacturing of fertilizers and secondly reforming the structure of agriculture. The major steps of reforms were abolition of Zamindari and controlling tenancy, the former assured cultivators full return to their labour and the latter assured certainty of occupation right for operating holdings. These were important but were not sufficient to transform Indian agriculture from being traditional to modern with improved technology. This outline in brief suggests that the missing step was finding for agriculture the required new technology that will help increase production rather rapidly. We had to wait for it till middle of sixties. We could hit upon the result of the search from abroad like Mexico for wheat revolution. The paddy was far behind. It came with major problem of acceptance by the consumer. But the science faculty rose to the occasion by applying their talent to fathom the required results.

End Note

1. The above picture is not quite unique for agriculture in India. Of course the countries in the Indian subcontinent share these characteristic in some measure. Vast area of the country heightens the unpredictability over the region as a whole. By nature, agriculture is dependent on weather, and hence most of the countries have to face in some measure the problem of low weather dependability.

3

Land and Water Resources

Two major, rather only, natural resources available for growing crops are land and water. We have dealt with the characteristics of land through the seeds and process of cultivation and processing of grains and other crops. Taste of grains adds one more dimension that affects the use of land. We shall examine the problem of land use subsequently. We first discuss availability of water and the role it plays in growing of crops.

We should remind ourselves at this stage that water supply is in two forms. We exclude ocean water because by its nature being saltish its use is restricted. Where the natural supply of water available through rainfall is low in quantity and less dependable in spread over the season, irrigation kicks in with a vital role to play.

Irrigation is an old time activity. It was recognized as essential during the Mohenjo-Daro and Harappan period and was located in drought prone area.[1] Weather in India is drought prone over much larger area. The drought prone area would account for almost 75% of the total cultivable area. It conveys that the need for irrigation is relatively much higher for crops grown in drought-prone area than for areas that receive normal rainfall. The latter is however not constant from one year to the next.

Around the same time irrigation appeared in different parts of the world. Initiative came independently from different area. Egypt, Iraq, Latin America, China had their independent systems of irrigation to meet their specific problems. The common feature was to divert water to farm land where natural supply was insufficient. Additional feature was to carry water over the heights through bamboos and buckets, a precursor of dams. Total irrigated area globally is still low around 17%. Against this the world population is continuously on rise, rather rapidly in recent times and mainly in developing nations. Thus, the stress is especially heavy in low income countries.

Agricultural revolution followed mainly in terms of seed selection and rotation and in England enclosure movement. All told, by year 1700 or later, agriculture became an occupation. Soon after, agriculture acquired some features of industry in nations then entering the phase of modernisation.

The history of agriculture and irrigation spread over centuries suggests that the effort to reap larger crop from the same land has been continuous for mankind. Our understanding of this process leads us to the pattern of combining inputs or the nature of production function.

It is understood that there is continuous effort to combine inputs including human labour in a manner that the point of combination gives the best results. This is the optimization of efficiency. Any change in that to further improve would result in less efficient use of inputs in relation to production. In other words, the point is optimum. A change in the combination of inputs or their total quantity of input would be acceptable only if it results into an improvement to prior position. In other words, the combination and level would give optimum output relating to inputs. Thus, it should improve efficiency of inputs. In other words, in three dimension graph the new optimum point lies above the previous optimum point.

What we derive is a production function by connecting the earlier optimum points prior to the present position. Another implication of the presentation is that the optimum combination of inputs at a given point in time represents the complementarity of inputs though the prior optimum points may suggest the relationship of substitution between inputs in a selected pairs or groups of inputs. We should grant at this point that the production function is representing the conditions at the selected location. The situation may vary from location to location. So if we consider varying locations at any given point in time we might get a production function over space. Locations of output from land at various points would then yield a production function over space. Unlike the historical production function, the production function over space would be a virtual presentation. The sum of these positions would end in a single point at any given point in time. These two production functions need to be differentiated[2].

The role that is played by prices of inputs needs to be examined. We begin with human labour a very important input. We go back to the combination of land and labour. As labour supply increases through population expansion, younger population that is dependent on adult population increases. Thus, the dependency ratio begins to rise. The adult population will have to put in more effort to have production sufficient to support the younger population beside the adult population. It may be difficult as is suggested by Malthus. In the era when land was not exhausted, expansion of production was possible by bringing in to cultivation virgin land with productivity being equal or higher. The process would come to an end as soon as the new land is exhausted. The process of bringing fallow land under cultivation and rotation of crops along side irrigation leads to double cropping. Taken as a whole, the picture would amount to combining more labour and irrigation with given area of land.

The scenario does not end here. The effort takes two forms, one, to match the production with the increasing population and two, to raise income level to the extent possible. The second form is an attempt to bring in an element of industry into agriculture. At this point, science begins to play a leading role. We then enter modernization by pursuing the goal of creating wealth rather than pursuing, 'produce to subsist'. At this stage, two classes emerge labour and land owner. Land becomes an asset to invest, irrigation emerges as an asset for production and alongside resources like fertilizer, etc. market produced inputs, obtained from markets flowing in from the manufacturing sector make an entry in the production system. Whatever is obtained from the market has to be paid out of sale of crops produced. Thus, the exchange of inputs obtained from outside the enterprise with the crops produced in the enterprise lead to the relative prices playing a distinct role.

This we shall still continue to name as traditional agriculture being at the stage before fertilizers and new seeds begin to have a distinct role. In this phase natural resources like land, irrigation and human labour will continue to play the major role. The phase of modern agriculture will take over when the role of natural resources declines and that of modern inputs mainly brought in from outside agriculture, increases. Tractors, chemical fertilizers and pesticides take the front seat in the modern agriculture. Additionally role of machines to replace labour increases significantly. The sequence may not be the same or similar. It will depend on developments in other sectors like industries, services, transport and research. Cities expand and rural areas shrink not in area but in terms of share in work force. Markets develop. For agricultural products, the demand from cities rises. And in response, production too increases.

If demand from cities or urban areas as a whole is close to zero, it will be the situation of extreme traditional agriculture. Such situation may arise rarely and could be in isolated communities, perhaps of tribals. At the other extreme, we might encounter a situation wherein the demand from urban areas is overpowering and a small share is retained in rural areas. It is not unlikely then that the farming will be like an industry.

In the latter case irrigation would play a stellar role accompanied by chemical fertilizers, pesticides, tractors and even harvesters. Transport and storage will be like silos and trucks. But the trend cannot be unending. The underground water available for irrigation is not limitless. The new methods of water management can help extend the resource available for irrigation up to a point. New research inflow can help produce larger harvests with the same amount of irrigation; over a period of few decades the bonus thus obtained can extend the course of development. We however see on the horizon a sharp line of restraint. The original Ricardian effect may kick in. It might operate at various levels. Land for farming is limited and continuous cultivation of the same land may bring in the adverse effect, which can be partially spared with such practices as rotational farming aided by wider distances between rows and water management like drip and sprinkler irrigation. All told, at some point Ricardian effect may overtake the beneficial effects of new research results. But this is a different type of Ricardian effect. The struggle between being in search of new technology and over exploitation of the traditional technology may oscillate between the Ricardian effect and shift of production function. The nature of change expected to give way to traditional agriculture will depend also on the general optimism based on human intellect leading to change based on research. One may say such optimism would suggest that the human intellect for bringing new levels of technology may be unlimited over a period of time. We have to take a long term view. As against this, the pessimistic view will suggest at least for short term that the talent requires time for all forces to play out. The period of intermission then could be trying, and unpreparedness will multiply the problems now faced. We recast the above proposition into production function frame.

We have two scenarios at this point. The new research results could be an infinite flow. We have to remove the constraint of time. If we have time constraint, then resourses and research results are not unconstrained. The former knocks off the basis of economic scenario where in we deal with scarcity of resources and choice from the limited resources at least at a point of time. The long term supply function has to be defined in the context of long term and not infinite time period. If there is a long enough pipeline and in the pipe line there are substitutable inputs available for producing crops, we have a potential for insubstitution. If the pipeline has no potential substitutable inputs, then the substitution possibilities are nearly absent. Estimates of factor substitution elastisities are based on the substitution available now, based on calculations on data now available. By definition this is a constrained function.

We are concerned with the elasticities of factor substitution or absence thereof to avail of full use of inputs/factors by substituting one in use by one which can be brought in use. Let us consider the case of irrigation and land. Punjab region has undergone a massive change in the use of irrigation. That leads us to observe substitution of land by water. But available data suggest a different picture. Subterranean water available for irrigation recedes at the rate of one foot per year. Whether the receding of water at the rate of one foot per year fully off-sets the substitution of land of the same quality is a matter of actual measurement, but data as they are available suggest the trend. The trend is that the substitution of land by water is less than the data would suggest. Based on this trend, we can observe that in farming, the economy would be down-treaded by complementarity except if the new resources are found as it happened in the case of oil and steel.

We may note at this stage the opposite trend in underground water for irrigation. The balance between the supply and demand for it leads to net loss leading to lowering of the level. As discussed earlier, this has happened in Punjab. During the last nine years, water level has gone down in Punjab at the rate of one foot per year. Two things have happened which has led to lowering of water level. Firstly, the area under irrigation has increased by drawing water from underground at a rate faster than the rate at which it is replenished by rain. Besides, the crops that are now grown in the same area use up more water. They are water intensive. Rice and wheat have replaced corn and barley and also cotton and groundnut that were quite common in years before Green Revolution. This is not the anathema of Punjab only. It is much more wide spread globally. USA also has experienced lowering of underground water. Here it could partly be the result of weather change. Rising temperatures would cause larger amount of water evaporation leading to less replenishment of water underground. This factor could eventually affect much vaster area of the globe.

In India, we have perennial rivers like Ganga (The Ganges). But the recent research suggests that the glaciers from which Ganga receives its water supply has undergone depletion. It could imply further receding of underground water in future.

Sum total of all the factors mentioned here would experience lower possibility of substituting land under crops by water. Following Ricardo, it would imply that the Ricardo effect of diminishing marginal product for land could set in via water depletion in the underground region. It would imply also that the phenomenon of complementarity would press heavily at an early stage.

We may return briefly to the demand for the product and its specific features. Demand for inputs are derived based on the demand for the product. Based on income level and on the relative price of the product, demand would affect the derived demand for inputs.

After the World War II, due to the rapid increase in incomes of those who participated in the market, the content of the demand changed. The demand shifted in favour of wheat and rice, fruits and vegetables, meat and milk. Most of these products required relatively more water to meet with the demand for these products. These products which are water intensive, consumed or needed more water for the same amount of product replaced by them. Here we consider millets which are being replaced by water intensive crops like wheat and rice. Rice has indirect effect. The nutritional value of plant material of millets is more compared to that of rice. Traditionally, cattle in rice growing regions are smaller in size and yield less milk. Ultimately, that would result in increased use of irrigation water per unit of output (such as calorie) and also for matching with growing demand for water intensive products. The receding of underground water observed in the Punjab area and also in UP which shifted its production in favour of sugar cane is the direct result of the phenomenon of the changing pattern of products grown. If the change in harvest composition continues, the stress on underground water may continue and even rise. There is every possibility of the process to rise undeterred. For the income level is rising and so also the shift in favour of demand for water intensive products may continue. The only check is the income elasticity of demand for quality of farm products. The income elasticity of demand for quantity of food like calories may rise at a declining pace while that for quality of food like taste and along with it the water use, may rise. Many of the water intensive crops have higher nutritive values too. But it would take us to yet another level of discussion viz. a comparative cost of nutrition for different products. Our main concern at this stage is the scarce resources like land and water may experience stress on the supply side while the income levels rise. The special case is of sugar cane. It is a three season crop, very intensive water-user and the product – sugar is low in nutrition. Besides, it may harm the health if consumed excessively and may lead to diabetes or aggravate it if the consumer has it already.

The resource inequity and the demand impacting on the supplies of input, resources may have to be considered further in one major way. When the developing economies enter the market scenario and the market favours the water intensive crops for transaction, those countries that import water intensive crops, in effect import water which is scarce in exporting countries. Since there is no overt transaction regarding water and it is implied in the relative price of the product like sugar or basmati rice and wheat it does not enter the calculations of the entrepreneur producing the crop. One major change that has taken place during the post-World War II is that international trade as a whole in farm products has rapidly increased mainly in terms of exports from developing economies. The governments of the low-income countries encourage the earning of foreign exchange to pay for the investment in capital goods that help modern industries. Even this scenario is undergoing further change with service sector expanding mainly based on electronics (IT).

We have considered the two major inputs land and water so far. The other major input is labour, the human aspect. We shall see in the interplay of other inputs, labour is trapped. We shall deal with it in the following chapter.

End Note

1. Region called Barmer located in Rajasthan receives rain once I seven years. This is an extreme case.

4

Production Relations

The post-World War II period witnessed many new developments. Among them is the rapid increase in the population. According to some estimates, the population of India may double in coming three to five decades. The world as a whole may have similar experience, the impact of which will be mainly in rural areas. Population growth is directly related to literacy and education level of mothers. Since literacy of girls is low in rural areas, population growth in rural areas in low income countries is relatively at a higher rate. The rural incomes depend heavily on agriculture and growth of agriculture is slow relative to growth of other two sectors. As a result, the growth of rural income is slow. Consequently, we find that the share of agriculture in Gross Domestic Product (GDP) is low and declining. The direct implication is that the farm population produces less for the exchange with non-farm sector products. It so happens that share of agriculture in GDP in India is between one third and one-fourth. Against this, the population engaged in agriculture is nearly half or more of the total working population in the country. That means every person employed in agriculture produces barely for one more person beside him or her-self. It is no wonder that level of living in rural areas measured in terms of non-food items consumed is much lower than that in urban or non-farm sector. This is the symptom of poverty as is commonly understood.

The reasons for poverty need to be investigated. The income is generated by employment. The first part is indicated before. The second part of employment generation needs to be indicated. Low employment in agriculture is not the result of less employment opportunity, but it is the part of factor relationship. If the factor substitution is low, even if there is enough labour force, the work force in employment may be low. For instance, if the rainfall is low and there are meager sources for irrigation, even if labour around is abundant those in labour force may constitute a small number. At this stage, we enter the production function make up.

Measurement of production function has seen three stages. In the early stage the C-D (Cobb-Douglas) was popular mainly because of its simplicity. It addressed one of the major requirements viz diminishing marginal product. But it went overboard. It resulted in elasticity of factor substitution not only fixed but quantitatively equal to ONE for all factors. This seems to be unrealistic. Especially in agriculture, land varies if at all within a narrow range compared to variations in other factors. The next achievement was in discovering a function known as CES (Constant Elasticity of Substitution.) It allowed the value of substitution elasticity to vary but continued to have the constraint of the value to be the same for all pairs of factors of production. While the C-D function has a long history, the CES has a small history beginning with sixties. Soon it was replaced by what came to be accepted as VES (Varying Elasticity of Substitution.) VES brings us closer to reality. Fitting functions of various shapes requires data to be used which reflect the past. In agriculture, the facts around the data change rather frequently. It did so rather rapidly in the near past due to the phenomenon of Green Revolution, which is now replaced by Continuous Green Revolution. Every change would affect the form and reality of the function. In turn, the power of projection will be weakened. This is inbuilt weakness of statistical form of function and data used for fitting the function. We are therefore back to square one at least in part. In the recent past, variations in certain facts like labour are autonomous in some respect. They do not follow exactly the Malthusian nor Ricardian formation. In part, population growth is independent of the demand for labour. Especially it is so in the post-World War II period.

The profession of agricultural economists for a while had a close relationship with Input-Output exercises. This formulation had a fixed relationship for an input and a product, the output. As product changed, so also the relation between input and output changed. The combination of various output for the same input gave a functional relationship between input and output. The same product will have different relationship between input and output. Leontief of MIT gave this form. It was then found soon after that the fixed relation between input and output is less realistic. Then followed nonlinear relationship between input and output. At an early stage, it was realized that as the variety of products increased, the statistical exercise became messier.

Thus, the production function exercise and input-output exercise has limited use. Both help us to understand the nature of the function in the immediate past and help us to project its outcome in the immediate future. More importantly, it helps us to understand the market efficiency or inefficiency if any, and would suggest if any correction is necessary and how it can be made.

We have to use one caution. What might seem to be inefficiency, might be due to market correction being attempted by individual entrepreneurs. By the time the correction is in place, the market may enter a new phase which may require further attempt for new corrections. The endless corrections may be the overt significance of dynamism of the market or efficiency of the response of the entrepreneur.

We leave behind the discussion of production function. It helps only in a limited way for understanding the problems of agricultural economics and the problems on the ground. And yet we cannot ignore the problems. One such problem is of employment and unemployment. I discuss that in the next chapter.

5

Employment and Unemployment in Agriculture

The ideal situation in agriculture existed long time ago. All those engaged in agriculture had their land and they worked on that land. They were concerned about the harvest. If production fell short of needs of those working on land, they would find additional land then not in use. If the land had low productivity, the new settlers would farm bigger areas.

The problem of employment came up after the existing land was brought under cultivation. The problem of employment has more than one angle. Since the family size may vary even before the labour market comes into existence, uneven demand for labour requires labour exchange or what is called involution. During the time of heavy demand for labour like harvest seasons, those who are under heavy pressure may request those with less pressure to help and may in return help the family that helped it in time of need. This arrangement has almost entirely disappeared by now.

Where tribals lived alongside others a trace of serfdom showed up. In south Gujarat (Surat) *Hali* system prevailed. Hali literally means one who ploughed land. The Hali system inculcated an element of serfdom. It would be initiated with borrowing. In most cases loan was borrowed initially for wedding. It was recovered by the land lord from the wages paid. The wage was inadequate to repay the loan with interest during the life time and sometimes heirs inherited the loan. Hali system prevailed in paddy area. The Hali system thus perpetuated the serfdom.

Tribals from Panch Mahals district (Gujarat) were recruited as semi serfs in Broach district. Cotton is a labour intensive crop and both districts Surat and Broach (Bharuch) wanted assured supply of labour. It could be had through serf or semi serf labour. Labour input was high but wages were low and hence income of labour was low. The serf labour slowly disappeared after rising of wages during the post World War II period and especially after the ushering in of Green Revolution.

Gujarat is mentioned as an illustration. The system seen in Gujarat was not an exception. Other states also had a prototype of this system. Within Gujarat state, mainly in Saurashtra before independence, in areas where princes ruled, trace of serfdom was seen. The system differed in content. And the labour intensive crop was not the major cause. What happened in Saurashtra happened in some of the Zamindari areas elsewhere. Uttar Pradesh had its share of labour employment system that tied labour to land. Bihar also shared the same system. Uttar Pradesh had a significant area under sugar cane. Sugar cane is a labour intensive crop.

We now come to the recent period. Subsequent to independence, Zamindari system was legally abolished by the Government. The reform was successful to a great extent. With that, the main core of labour market changed. Demand and supply determined wages. This did not imply that the wage was sufficiently high for labour to subsist.

Concepts and Measurement

Even when labour market emerged in agriculture, its character remained distinct from that of organized labour. We have come to accept labour as fully employed when the employee works for eight hours a day. And according to implicit contract, the employee has week ends free as paid holiday. Sunday is accepted as a paid holiday and Saturday employment varies, it is half day or alternate week holiday. In addition all bank holidays are paid holidays for the organized labour. It makes easy for such organized labour to have statistics of employed labour.

In agriculture and other unorganized labour, conditions may vary. Employment in agriculture is guided by seasons. During busy seasons like sowing, weeding and harvesting hours of work may stretch from eight to even fourteen. The employment with long hours may or may not be continuous. During off season employment may be for fewer hours. The employment pattern may vary for owner and wage paid labour. Work for part of the day would be a usual pattern for owner. Wage-paid labour may have full time employment for the days when they are employed for most of the time. Pattern also included half day for work. But for owners, the flexibility varied. Members of family may join the work force often irrespective of the individual needs like attending school or need for rest due to age or health conditions. During off-season, this flexibility resulted in working for less than eight hours a day. But it may not be exactly half a day of four hours.

We can thus see three attributes for rural employment. Hours, days and the number of members of the family drafted in the work force. Mostly the decision is taken by the head of the family. The head will decide on the basis of the need. During the rush season, the head may decide to recruit most if not all members of the family including females, children, old and sometimes even invalid sick members. Children may have to skip school and sick persons may have to draw on their energy level which may already be low. Ladies members may have to work in addition to their regular work in kitchen, bathing tiny tots and taking care of those who are bed-ridden. For each participating member, the head decides for which day he or she will work and on the day he or she works, for how many hours individual will work. From this scattered record, the data are integrated to get the picture of employment, unemployment and partial employment. Unemployment is defined for the period for which the workforce participant is available for work but has no work. This is a weak definition. During off season most of those who were active, including women and old persons with low energy level, would have a desire to have work but their desire is to work at wages which reflect shadow wage level for which according to them they will be willing to give up their leisure time. This could be about the half or more of the wage they earned during the peak season. But employers will not be willing to offer. For workers, the reservation wage level will be above the efficiency level. The reservation wage level suggests the level of wage at which the worker will be willing to offer him herself to be in the labour force

Since for collecting data at the field, question asked may not fully bring out the nuance of the wage level involved. It is not unlikely that the rural unemployment based on field data may have an element of overstating the reality. We would grant the fact that wage level desired could be higher than the market level, which would imply that the rural wages may be less satisfying. This is desired or reserved versus legitimate level may land us in human[1] versus economic wages. For this debate there cannot be a satisfactory solution. Over a period of time if wages are rising, as they did during the period of Green Revolution, the gap between human versus economic wages may be eroded and even bridged.

The major problem of rural wages is thus unclear and hence also of measuring employment and unemployment. Long time back during decade of depression, Gandhiji tried to solve it by introducing spinning wheel. His basic argument was that basic needs of a family may be met by self help and not by market economy. Basic needs would include food and clothing and in some respect pottery for making tiles, some storage vessels for the house. Even dung cakes may be made to supply fuel or manure or both. The dung was emphasized also for supporting good harvest. It was thus indirect help. Much of the unemployment or seemingly leisure time during the non-peak season may thus be used in self-employment and the material produced by family would add to the family income. Of course in the Gandhi's formulation, an element of politics was involved. Khadi replaced partly the foreign cloth and thus saved foreign cloth imported mainly from Manchester and Lancashire in U.K. Khadi movement was complemented by Swadeshi movement. It shifted the demand for imported cloth to homemade or by national textile industry. Both resulted in increased employment, the former in rural areas and the latter in urban sector. Both these survived during the depression decade. After independence, the emphasis on Swadeshi declined. Even the manufacturing pattern in U.K. changed. Textile industry moved to less developed countries.

What is important to note is that agriculture has peak and non-peak seasons and that affects employment. After Green Revolution, the employment increased dramatically in areas that took to labour intensive crops. Even with the new cropping pattern following Green Revolution, seasonality continued but with reduced impact. The steep increase in demand for labour led to movement of labour from low demand to high demand areas. The specific case is of labour from Bihar seeking employment in Punjab and parts of UP. This movement of labour partially smoothened the unevenness of seasonality but did not fully remove it. This problem of seasonality is part of agriculture and few other small scale industries in rural and even to an extent in urban areas. The problem is: can we eliminate it so that employment is smooth and continuous? It does not seem to be likely. And hence the need seems to have arisen for schemes like EGS (Employment Guaranteed Scheme). This was initiated first by Maharashtra State (V.S. Page) but is now a part of planning under the management of the central government. Such scheme taken up by the state would involve working with a formulae for just implementation like how much employment to be generated and what type of employment will be generated, like road construction, etc. Formula will be involved in selecting location which should be within five kilometers.

Hitherto we have demonstrated that seasonality is a part of employment pattern in agriculture. When machines such as tractors, harvesters and pump irrigation enter agriculture the seasonality in employment is partially smoothened. However, as long as there is unevenness in employment over seasons within a year, the problem of measurement of unemployment in agriculture will continue to be less satisfactory.

Currently National Sample Survey (NSS) agency is the primary agency for data collection. A workforce participant working for more than four hours is reported as fully employed for that day and those reporting less than four hours on a given day are reported to be employed for half day. Housewives would work for less than four hours during the non-peak season and thus work put in by them may not be reported as full employment.

There is yet another glitch which should be noted. During the harvest season most of the self employed workers would tend to put in more than eight hours. This additional period of employment above eight hours on a given day will be skipped in records. We have a record suggesting this pattern. Initially, the NSS reported hours worked for employed persons and not days worked. Taking hours of employment and converting them into 8-hour days of employment would give the days of full employment equal to days of work put in organized sector of economy. This is a picture very much different from the current picture of recorded days of employment. It is true that those reporting unemployed for half day for the day because they have worked for less than four hours could be set off against those working for more than four hours and thus the major tradition of rounding off the data will be satisfied, but may not reflect reality. And as I pointed out above, the longer hours of work during the busy season may go unreported.

This discussion is not for satisfying measurement only. Non-seasonal unemployment had at one time given rise to serious theory of development, theory based on utilizing unemployed labour out of agriculture. We shall deal with glitches in theory as such later.

We should deal with one more widely prevalent proposition at this stage. It is suggested that surplus/surfeit of unemployment in agriculture would imply that labour should be moved to industrial sector or even services sector. This I have mentioned earlier. A detailed and critical look into this proposition would suggest not only massive investment in industries or services sector but also in infra-structure like transport and other related activities. The latter may outweigh the former. Recent example is one of serious shortage of drinking water in Mumbai and serious restrictions proposed to meet with the problem. Mumbai is one such example. Kolkata is yet another. Recently the problem of drinking water for Chennai was addressed by a private initiative. (Sri Sathya Sai Central Trust.[2] These are tips of the problem. Small towns and cities too have water and sanitation problems. The agencies dealing with this aspect do not have enough resources. Add to this the problem of providing education and health and electricity for homes and industries and we can see the giant of inadequate urban facilities raising its head. If we succeed in moving rural population to urban areas even partially, we will end up in a large amount of slums like Dharavi slums[3] in Mumbai. Slums are like boils on urban body. Kolkata has many such boils causing concern to all conscientious persons. In big cities like Mumbai and Kolkata part of the labour population lives on sidewalks (footpaths) with no cover in winter and no protection from rain in monsoon season, besides absence of water and sewer facility accepted as minimum civil facilities. For people living on sidewalks, kitchen and bed rooms are together in open sidewalks. Dwellings will be in many cases even inferior to poor housings in rural areas. Thus, employment creation may turn out to be a super human problem especially if it is to be addressed within short period. India has seen 7 10 per cent annual rate of growth for the national economy as a whole but growth for agriculture has remained stuck to 2-3 per cent. Against this disparity, the population growth in rural areas has continued to be uncomfortable more so in rural areas. Thus, the problem of rural-urban disparity may continue to strangle the rural areas for a long time if the present approach is continued. A new approach has to be evolved in which rural areas receive major attention. Before we examine the new approach we shall look into poverty, the major anathema of rural life especially in the developing economies. Even before that we have to examine a special aspect of employment and unemployment in agriculture.

Moving out of agriculture or rural areas as a whole in pursuit of employment for villages in deep rural areas is not smooth and related only to the wage rate. Wage rate may be sensitive to developing technology like Green Revolution. The labour intensive technology may lead to a rise in wages. To such achievement, labour may respond from low wage area to rising wage area. As already mentioned in the recent past, we have seen such movement of labour from rural Bihar to rural Punjab. But additional factor that may need to be considered is the structure of labour employment. The tribal labour may face constraint in resorting to migration. Such constraint may delay the movement to the extent that the upsurge in wage may subside before the tide in the labour migration sustains. There is yet another point which is important and that needs to be considered. The cost of migration and settling in a distant place requires financial backing and human contact. In regard to both these, the poor labour families might face serious obstacles. There may be yet another factor. Cultural values need to be considered. For instance among certain castes like Rajputs, working in fields by women is unacceptable. It is nearly a taboo. Even if males migrate, females may not migrate with them. The gender-differential may result in income differential. All these factors may be intermediate ones, as the time passes by, their impact may gradually wane. Good education and better choice for food and other articles for living in urban areas may provide a stronger motivation for migration to urban areas. From this point of view, the attraction may be more for the metro urban areas. The construction work may generate massive employment opportunities on temporary basis. Here the labour may not be provided with housing.

Before we leave the study of employment we would be required to examine the aspect of rural poverty. Then as a solution to these aspects we shall examine the possibility of revised approach to the problem of rural employment and income. I take up poverty aspect in next chapter. I feel that the rural employment problem is in essence a problem of low income and associated poverty. Next chapter deals with the essence of the problem.

End Notes

1. Human wages would at least match with the wage that would give food enough to cover the energy production required for work to be put in. Economic wages would suggest where market would match supply and demand for labour.
2. Sri Sathya Sai Central Trust was founded by Sri Sathya Sai Baba in September 1972. Under his guidance, the Trust has undertaken a number of welfare activities such as providing free education at Sri Sathya Sai Schools and the Institute of Higher Learnings, delivering quality medical care at primary, secondary and tertiary levels completely free of charge, supply of pure drinking water in various regions of Andhra Pradesh loveing a population of over 3 million people and to the city of chennai with a population of over 10 million.
3. Slum Dog Millionaire, a film based on life in Dharavi slums. The efforts are underway for removing such slums and replacing them by regular apartment houses.

6

Rural Poverty - Roots and Structure

Rural society has historically a structure of its own. The structure changes at its own pace. Unequal incomes emerge from this changing structure. Poverty has its roots in this process.

Agriculture is historically based on land and labour, the two major inputs given basically by nature. Investment in both improves quality of both. With increase in labour force, the cultivable land gets exhausted. Further expansion of labour at uneven pace impinges unevenly on land ownership. To begin with, the families with large size have an advantage. When labour is in short supply and land is yet not fully exhausted, the land holding can be large in possession of large families. We need not assume the same amount of skill level and same effort level in all labour units. Besides, the advancement based on improved technology depends in agriculture on biological advancement. This is slow and is based on some uncertain factors. It is unlike the mechanical advancement. With expanding labour force, mechanical assets can be expanded almost at the same rate and the level of full employment can be pursued. With expanding employment, incomes may tend to increase, especially so, if mechanical advancement makes possible substitution of labour. In traditional agriculture, animal power helped substitute man-power. Here we see opportunity for factor substitution in favour of physical assets or what we would like to call factor substitution in favour of capital. The investment in assets makes possible to earn income from non-labour sources. In agriculture, this stage, is difficult early enough. It may set in at a late stage. Agriculture remains a labour intensive activity for a long time and continues to be so if rural labour continues to expand at a rate faster than additional land can be brought under cultivation. Beside land and labour, water in the form of irrigation is an essential input. It helps substitute dry land and helps provide additional employment to labour. Thus, irrigation helps agriculture to be labour intensive.

Technological change may be in the form of improved seeds and bringing into production process, chemical fertilizers along with insecticides. The major technological change in terms of improved seed became possible with the help of development in statistical science. And statistical science advanced with the help of development of theory of probability. The theory helped make seed selection scientific. Major development took place in this direction in early 1930s. More important development after seed selection was crossbreeding. That was a pure scientific development based on biological science. Maize or corn was the first one to be impacted. The new research made a huge impact in USA by middle or late 1930s. The Green Revolution made an entry much later some time in 1960s. In terms of spread of technological improvement and its extension to new areas was the major development. This development took place as the growth in population speeded up in the post-World War II period. USA experienced during this period what is now known as baby boom in population growth. In India, the rate of growth of population crossed two percentage points. The race between the agricultural production and growth of population gradually turned in favour of population leading to increased per capita output of agricultural commodities. By then Malthusian proposition was left in background.[1] We should keep in mind that the agriculture accepts new technology with lags. Population growth rate too declines after a lag. Between the two, the decline of rate of growth of population decline is slower.

The demand for agricultural commodities plays a role that directly affects the measurement of poverty rate in the community. The demand for agricultural commodities depends on two factors. One factor is growth of population. This factor was dominant during the post-World War II period. With each decade, the rate of growth of population tended to decline and hence the effect of the population factor also tended to decline. The decline set after the Green Revolution in India had made a major advance.

The second factor, beside population that affects the demand is income. Incomes tended to increase at a faster rate with the planning for growth. But at the same time, the income elasticity of the basic goods would tend to decline. The opposite effects of the two, rise in income and decline in the income elasticity, have a picturesque impact. The population growth starting at the higher level declines gradually. The effect of such factors as education level especially of girls and improved health has opposite effects. Increased education leads to decline in the rate of growth of population but improved health would lead to the increase in population. The second is caused by reduction in death rate at a faster rate than the decline in the rate of births in the community. When the rate of growth of population slows down and the rate of growth of production continues to dominate, the demand will tend to rise; but the rise will be contained by reducing income elasticity. This is the general law that the income elasticity of necessities tends to decline as income increases. Thus, on the whole, the pressure of demand for agricultural commodities might tend to decline.

The crux then lies with supply behaviour. The technological change may raise supply at a faster rate when new technology is introduced. Two factors need to be considered. We are familiar with learning curve. Learning curve implies that relatively more enterprising producers may adopt the rewarding technological improvement at first, followed by slow adopters. Laggards may adopt the improved technology last. Thus, between the enterprising and laggards, there could be relatively big time gap. The laggards may thus be caught in low income level and may be stuck for a while below the poverty level, if they happened to be in the poverty stratum. Resources may be in low supply and from it the enterprising farmers draw for their use. If it happens, the laggards may be hurt further.

Thus, the demand and supply patterns may affect the income levels of different strata of farmers differently in rural areas especially during the transition from old to new technology.

In the overall picture the supply behaviour as a result of technological change may press on the demand pattern. This needs to be considered very carefully. The incomes in rural communities may be affected by and finally adjusted by transfer of labour from rural to urban areas. This pattern has led to reduced share of labour in rural areas over time. This is very much apparent in developed countries. Workers employed in rural areas in USA are very low, around 3 % of the total work force. Similar picture obtain in developed countries of Europe.

At this stage, we have to deal with one major point pertaining to developing nations. They experience from time to time shortage of basic goods mainly food and other agricultural commodities like sugar, edible oil, etc. Two factors can be identified for this effect. These countries achieve higher level of GDP. India provides an example. The industrial growth hovers round 10 % per annum in India and service sector experienced growth around 15 %. Against this, agriculture achieved between 2 to 3 % per annum. The average for agriculture of 2 to 3 % would put agricultural sector in the trap of poverty, especially the labour working in agriculture.

Beside, the improvement in technology is less likely to be evenly spread. The areas that have a disadvantage to begin with, may experience further disadvantage. The drought prone areas are among them. The individual cases may be identified. In the year of low rainfall and hence of low output, the poor producers may be hard hit. One such year may put them at the risk of losing the land owned and cultivated mainly by self labour. They may be then pushed down to landless labour or to the class of small holders. Or they may be tenants next year leasing in land and using their labour for the lessor. In either case, they may be at greater disadvantage regarding returning to the original status. If the land is mortgaged, the cultivators involved in mortgage will have to return not only the principal but also will have to pay interest. If they are lucky and harvest is good, they might come out of the hole in which the bad harvest put them.

In the context of the technological change, there might be a few overoptimistic entrepreneurs who might put at stake the capital beyond their savings and if they are caught by greedy traders they might loose their total savings and land themselves in debt heavy enough to ruin their enterprise. Then they become desperate and in some cases even commit suicide. They sometimes value more their reputation than their finances. Their family would land themselves in poverty from which they may not come out soon or even any time.

Reputation is a social factor and such social factor works in more than one ways. A social event like death in the family, wedding or the like may prompt the sufferers to borrow to meet the unexpected commitment. Poverty may then be the end result. Such social factors have lost their impact over time. New factors have emerged. Instances of parents financing their children for sending them to expensive educational institutions like medical colleges and engineering colleges or even financing the migration to foreign countries are now common. While children may benefit in these cases, but parents may have to shed their valuable capital including land.

Thus we see that poverty has many prongs, and once these prongs hit a family, poverty may seem to be an unending curse. Even during such hard times, the really judicious persons may benefit by the technological change. The growth of agriculture on one hand and push of technological change on the other, finally lead the rural prosperity. But the migration to urban areas would be the deciding factor for sizable and lasting prosperity of rural areas. The two aspects of agricultural economics taken together, viz. employment and poverty lead us to conclude that low-income rather than unemployment seems to be the harder problem to overcome.

Further, what seems to be employment problem is indeed the problem of income or earnings capacity. Providing employment through state supported projects at wages which are not on match with the reserve rate, the labour is faced with a difficult choice to deny the opportunity for employment which does not ensure the wage needed for them to subsist at above poverty level, and accepting living under the poverty line. The farmer and labour behaviour is in favour of the former and not the latter. Then the leisure time opted for by working group of labour would seem to accept overt leisure time termed as unemployment for them.

One more aspect of poverty identification may be considered at this stage. It resembles the type of problem faced regarding uncovering the real unemployment against the choice for leisure. This is the demand aspect. When incomes rise, we considered that the income elasticity would tend to decline. That is an overall position. The food as a commodity has two aspects. They are quantity and quality. For defining poverty and then measuring the extent of poverty in a community, level of calorie intake is taken as the basis and it is then related to the income level per adult.

The logic implied is that there is a minimum level of calorie required for reasonable health condition and certain level of income is required to permit that much calorie consumption. Up to this level, the logic seems to be persuasive. But the economics of the poverty level will want us to take into account the behavior of the individual regarding selection of food for consumption. At least there are two aspects to the behaviour. Calorie-intake as quantity of food based on logic mentioned above and quality as apart from quantity. Calorie may be obtained from various types of food. Calories obtained from grain would be less expensive compared to calories obtained from milk, meat or fruit and vegetables. The income elasticity for calories would tend to decline as incomes rise, but income elasticity for quality of food may tend to rise at least near the poverty line. The end result would be that the calories consumed may rise rather slowly and hence the decline in the extent of poverty may be slow. So long as the demand for quality of food tends to rise, the phenomenon of slow decline in the extent of poverty may continue. This would be true at least in developing economies at the present stage. It is likely that efforts to raise incomes may not directly help in reducing the extent of poverty substantially.

Non-grain food is not always quality food in terms of better nutrition like milk or vegetables. Of late, we find in remote rural areas certain foods. Soft drinks like Coca Cola occupying a village shop front corner. And Coca Cola is not food that would add substantially to the nutrition level. But it would add to the cost of food intake. Prior to Coca Cola, tea stalls had made an entry into villages. They have not given up their pride of position. It added to the earnings of the stall owners but did not add visibly to nutritional quality of food. These foods can better be described as 'status food' for a class of people. The status food would include expensive foods like milk, meat, fruit and vegetables. They may be desirable from nutrition angle but they add an unaccounted angle to measuring poverty levels. All these illustrations would show that status foods like quality food would tend to raise the income elasticity of demand for food. As such, it would further deter the speed with which the decline in expenditure on food as a whole is expected. While tea stall with snacks continued to be small enterprises, the soft drinks made possible for corporations to gain foot holds in the rural society. This is far away from the dreams of leaders like Gandhi which he depicted in his famous work 'Hind Swaraj'. The leader like Gandhiji would look for increased economic independence while the development now taking place will take the rural society in the opposite direction. I shall deal with this aspect of economic development later.

We have looked into both demand and supply aspects of food consumption and the effect of both on the economic conditions of the rural economy. We can now bring them together. Supply of food would depend on the level of technology like hybrid corn, etc. and also on the cropping pattern. Cropping pattern would include non-food crops or what may be called commercial crops like cotton, oil seeds, sugar and fabrics such as jute. They are grown in different parts of the country and many of them have specific parts of the nation convenient for them to grow. For instance, jute is grown in the north eastern part, basically West Bengal and Assam. Cotton is concentrated in western part and part of Karnataka State. Sugar cane is basically grown in Maharashtra and U.P. Their expansion will affect local cropping pattern. Expansion of commercial crops would imply a possible reduction in the area under food grains and sometimes pulses. The total earnings may tend to increase and so also the intake of food may increase from the demand side.

The consumption pattern may also impact the cropping pattern. With rising of incomes of rural population, the status food grains like rice and wheat may find a growing importance in the food consumption pattern even in areas where they are not grown. The areas where they are grown will then find increased market for their output. In the areas where rice and wheat are not grown but consumption gains the marketed surplus of minor food grains may tend to decline. The net effect of the opposite effects may be less predictable. It will depend on income levels. On the whole after Green Revolution, the supply mainly of superior grains like rice and wheat has tended to increase and that of minor grains may tend to decline, and the marketed surplus may tend to rise. This phenomenon of rising marketisation may affect the entire pattern of agricultural production.

Marketisation has also the influence transferred from international trade. India became a food surplus country in the wake of Green Revolution. This was a marginal gain. Wheat and rice have been exported. The growth of exports has been slow. And sometimes it is volatile. During the years of low production the surplus may turn into deficit. This is the transition stage. The steady export is the next stage and it will be achieved after the production level is stabilized at a higher level.

I shall deal with the international trade in detail in the following chapter. I shall also deal with the terms of trade and their impact on the crop production level and pattern. We may, however, observe at this stage that the country may possibly move forward to rapid urbanisation and the rural urban relationship may so change that agriculture begins to lose its relative position in terms of share of workforce in agriculture compared to that in non-agriculture sectors. The developed countries like UK and USA are in this stage, agriculture in both of them have a slender share of labour in agriculture compared to that in non-agricultural sectors. Other developed countries are in similar stage. For India as we have seen, this is, a far off stage for reasons already mentioned. Urbanisation based on rural out-migration at a pace sufficient to cause a decline in the percentage of labour in agriculture in the meanwhile may face certain formidable obstacles.

End Note

1. Malthusian proposition surfaced in recent times in the context of natural resources like petrol, minerals such as iron, etc. Increased use would deplete these natural sources without replacing them.

7

Terms of Trade and Marketisation

Terms of trade are mainly the outcome of market participation. Barter transactions did exist before formal marketing took over, but these transactions had severe limitations of distance and time. The transaction took place in the designated market area in most cases. They were valid at the time of concluding the transaction. These limitations put severe restriction on the amount that was transacted and the exchange rate such transaction threw up. The entry into market relaxed formally the limitations of time and space. However, the informal transaction on barter basis continued. It is fresh in our memory that peddlers went round a group of villages and sold their wares like toys or specified vegetables, etc. They would have food grain in return of their wares. This type of transactions facilitated broadening the variety of contents of consumption basket with some wares added in it. The local consumers would part with their goods mostly the staple food grain which they had a surplus supply. Because of its limitations, the system dwindled in its size and finally disappeared. The content of transaction obviously varied depending on the local supply and needs of the buyer and seller for goods for their consumptions. It is still remembered by many that tribals would exchange salt for precious gems.

The former would be made available by outsiders well versed in the values of gems and local tribals would willingly exchange their possessions for which they would have lower values in their calculations against salt for they lived deep in forest away from sea shores. From their residence, the salt would be nearly inaccessible. But are gone such days. The means of transport expanded and with them the information needed for fair transactions increased.

The background given above prepares us for the terms of trade for agriculture and its implications. The 'terms of trade' not favourable to agriculture could imply that the agricultural sector has to part with relatively larger amount of goods produced by it and thus the income and hence also the consumption is limited by the relative terms of trade. This logic was extended to imply that unfavourable terms of trade would reflect the existence of poverty in agriculture. This assumption is acceptable in limited sense. Let us examine this twist.

Let us take the effect of weather first. A good weather may give bumper harvest. Whether the income would rise as much depends on price elasticity of demand for food grains and other crops. Low price elasticity may lead to lower total revenue, and total costs not being lower may result in lower incomes for agriculture. If agriculturists carry debt burden from the past, the repayment of these debts in kind or cash may further depress prices. During this period of bumper crop, the incomes of non-agricultural sector may be down because there may be less demand for their products. The final result will depend on the capacity of each sector to hold on to the inventory. If agriculturists decide to withhold relatively larger portion of their harvest for the next year as back up for possible low harvest, then the market may have the same or lower flow of product entering the market.

Marketable Surplus

Here we should take up the discussion about the marketable surplus and its impact on the market attributes and prices. In a country like India, taking a look at the pre-

Green Revolution period, we will find that the marketed surplus hovered around 20% of the total food grain production. Take an example of low harvest year. Production is down by, say, 2%. The impact of low harvest then would be dwindling of marketed surplus by 10% if the producers do not part with the harvest by cutting down their consumption. In a country and at a time the production barely met the basic need, lower marketable surplus may create scarcity condition out of proportion compared to the decline in overall production. In the market, lowering of supply by 10% would imply increase in prices of food grain by 20%.We assume here 0.5 to be the supply elasticity for supply coming to the market. This jacking up of the prices may be entirely by operation of market forces only. The impact may be uneven between the harvest prices and the off season prices. We might experience a shade of draught year if not famine year even though the production in the year concerned is down by 2%. If the production is down by 10% and marketed supply is slim to 50%, the prices may double and poor sections of population may experience scarcity verging on famine. This is not to suggest that better entitlement arrangements can help mightily the situation, but in its absence the hardship may be so deleterious that a section of the community may find it difficult to survive through the year. India had a history in the past of frequent famines, and the famine of 1942 stands out among them. Not only there was absence of robust arrangement for entitlements to save human lives but also in addition to worsen the already bad situation the government entered the market and cornered from already low supplies a sizeable portion for military purposes.

Our intention here is to show that agricultural sector has built in it the kinks that twist the operation of market forces. Other factors contribute to the twist. The trading community may use their monopolistic position to take advantage of unfavourable market condition. The role of marketing agency aggravates the bad situation but the cause lies elsewhere.

The fact that the production level is affected by weather which in itself is erratic leads to aggravation of the volatility of price levels from year to year. In addition to entitlement, we may therefore need arrangements to reduce market volatility by managing the stocks of grain. In my view, the stocks can be better managed at producers level than at the bureaucratic level. But this conclusion may have to be examined in depth.

We have experience of both price control to protect the interest of consumers and price-support to help farmers in India. Most developed nations have income support or price support. The latter is the reflection of.the basic weakness of agriculture. Agriculture is labour intensive. Besides, labour does not get continuous employment. Labour is thus not only the major part of inputs and employment is unpredictable but also the income of owners who supply labour have erratic levels. The income level in agricultural sector is found to be below the income level of labour in non-agricultural sector. The labour supply is generated primarily through the natural growth of population and mainly in rural areas, especially when the rural sector is overwhelmingly large. If employment opportunities are not adequate, we expect emerging of unemployment as an immediate consequence.

Here we should consider the long term consequence as well. Emergence of unemployment could depress wages. As a result, opportunity to invest emerges. It is more likely that returns to investment in capital and rent of land under cultivation may be higher relative to wages. Those having surplus funds or credit can decide to invest. In the long run, the new technology or improved capital may lift the level of technology and as a result production level. Here is the window for increased employment in agriculture. There can be trend towards finding employment for surplus labour that might have emerged as a result of population growth. Thus, full employment is not inaccessible.

The problem may be complicated in terms of time taken for the process of adjustment of factor inputs in response to increase in labour as a natural process. It will not be instantaneous and during the intervening period, the labour may continue to grow. The entire process may be unending unless the natural growth of population begins to adjust to the changing proportions of factor inputs and also to the changing level of technology.

We left the discussion about the marketable surplus where we considered the process of mutual adjustment of factor inputs. The release of supply into the market will depend on the price elasticity and the production level. We have assumed price elasticity to be 0.5. But if it turns out to be lower, say, 0.2 the surplus brought to market in a year of production being lower by 2% will be around 50% lower. The urban demand being what it is, there would be near famine conditions. We have experienced in 2009-2010 the skyrocketing of prices. This phenomenon can be partially attributed to low production, low price elasticity and public sector storage level unchanged.

We may consider at this stage international or global terms of trade. Here we have an additional factor to consider. Global price may be one but those who bring their produce to international market may not have comparable take-home price of the product. Most developing nations may have lower wage rates, but they do not have comparable level of technology and they have relatively poor infrastructure. Thereby, they have relatively expensive transport and even storage facilities. Transport may be more time consuming for given distance. Costly transport might add to the cost and lower the take home price. Banking system may be inadequate. That too may make marketing expensive and deterring. When all factors are weighed, the advantage in favour of developing nations may be slim. Besides, the capacity to store for following years would be very limited.

The developed nations may have some indirect advantages too. Some of the servicing institutions would be operating in highly developed form like insurance, shipping, banking, etc. and increased international trade may add to the incomes of these agencies engaged in international trade.

The service sector and the manufacturing sector may also benefit from increased trade. These indirect benefits may not be reflected in the terms of trade considered usually. The manufacturing sector may be highly advanced and its advantage over the agricultural sector as a whole may be much more in developed countries. Considering all these factors, the advantage of developing nations may be limited. There may be one overt advantage. Market may be very limited in the developing nations and expansion of market through international market may add to the advantage. (Experience of Mexico)

How the advantage of developing countries may be derided is seen through the history of imperial era. In India, the exchange rates were manipulated through the political super power. Even railway rates were manipulated against the raw material producers. This became so evident that political movements were staged against the ruling powers. Various methods were employed in ruled countries by the empires. In India, the side effect was advantage of developed railway system, extension of crops such as cotton, jute and even indigo before the First World War. The gain was not without the cost weighing against it.

The present period viewed from the global trade has greater advantage, but disadvantage is increased volatility of prices and off take in the market leading to unpredicted shortages from time to time.

The developing nations may find it difficult to cope up with oscillating situations of probable surplus to probable shortage. Exports in one year may turn into imports in some years.

8

Capital Formation in Agriculture

The post-World War II period had an emphasis on economic development. It was an outcome of two forces, firstly, the developing economies were steeped in poverty and population was expanding rapidly. Expansion of population was independent of economic considerations. The development of chemicals such as DDT helped control rage of malaria which expanded the life span. Secondly, such chemicals as DDT and antibiotics helped save life from deadly diseases in general. Their development snapped the slim relation between production of food and population. The independence of population growth of economic factors, further led to stress on economic conditions in developing nations. The condition was so bad that the developing nations were addressed as backward countries. Setting up of international institutions like World Bank, FAO and IMF and even ILO led to the change in nomenclature from backward to undeveloped and later to developing nations. During this period it was universally accepted that the development of backward economies had the highest priority. But we would add the technological level as a factor to aid development more so in agriculture, since the major factor land is fixed in quantity and its substitution is inevitable for rapid growth. Substitution is made possible by irrigation, fertilizers and land development like gully plugging, land levelling, and also deeper ploughing. Increased production is possible essentially by changing the biological base, namely, by evolving new seeds with better potential for production.

The technical level is raised through focused research. The developing economies were engaged initially in improving the structure through land reforms thinking that changes in rights to land would enable improving the production potential. This logic worked on margin. Major technological change in the pipe line makes possible rather rapid shift in technological level. Return being higher, it motivates producers to invest in new inputs like manufacturing or importing or fertilizers. The new technology often requires a bundle of new inputs including irrigation and hence larger investment. Thus, technological change promotes investment.

There could be mistakes in judgment and consequent misjudgment in investment. Here is an example of Punjab. Farmers invested in tube wells, the depth of which was just right for the current use. When all began digging to reach water level, the available water level receded and thus some of the wells dried up. Farmers had to dig still deeper to reach the receded level of water. The misjudgment was in collective action. Additional investment required was primarily for maintaining the production level. Since water drawn from tube wells was unchanged and cost had increased, irrigation costs increased. Hence the cost per unit of output increased.

The price support programme that had the goal of supporting prices to cover the cost of production with normal profit was badly hit. The price support programme was hit otherwise also. The self employment was included in the cost. It is claimed that self employment does not land itself to easy evaluation for cost. So also rental value of owned land may thwart the cost calculations.

Let us leave aside the price support programme as such but liberal payment for covering costs may add to the profits and that may erroneously add to the motivation of investment in capital. Digging too many tube wells in a given area could be partly the result of such decision.

Thus, capital formation could be overestimated and the true measurement may be erroneous. This happens when technological change is rapid and too tempting.

One general observation would be in place at this stage. The traditional agriculture had a low C/O (capital-output) ratio close to -1. The ratio moved up with introduction of the new technology. The new seeds made it possible to take two crops in a year, Kharif (monsoon) crop followed by Rabi (Winter) crop. But that required land to be prepared for second crop in a relatively short time. It would not be possible to complete land preparation for second crop like wheat by manual labour over the entire land to be ploughed. It became necessary to mechanize the process. Investment in tractor was the only way out. Investment increased and so also the C/O ratio. Capital formation followed till it ended with the harvester on relatively larger holdings. The process of agriculture being capital intensive, thus followed. It is slow because most of the holdings are still small or medium size. With expansion of labour slowing down and outflow of labour picking up speed, the process of capital intensity too may pick up speed. We would be moving away from labour intensive to capital intensive agriculture with modernization. This may happen initially with the areas with potential for irrigation, but the other areas too may be brought in the process when new seeds are discovered for dry areas. The corn (or maize) is very much in the line for modernization more for its use for making bio-fuel as well as making paper in developing nations. Bajara, Jowar and Ragi have their alternatives with greater production potential. But the strain newly brought in has smaller spectrum with the result there is danger that if the crop is affected by a disease or insects, the entire crop over the area may be seriously damaged. Besides, the old strains have potential for resisting the virulent enemies to the crop. The taste factor that supports the taste for the locally grown cereals is also very much present. These factors may slow down the process of modernization in the area growing minor cereals.

To conclude we observe that agriculture responds to the economic impulses. It is comfortable with technological changes. Operation of economic forces is further helped by changing level of technology.

I have concentrated in this chapter on capital formation in the context of modernization of agriculture. The reason is obvious. In the context of traditional agriculture we have noted that the factor substitution was low close even to zero. This is supported by a few scattered researches. The modernization supports factor substitution. As pointed out above, the substitution is mainly capital on one hand and other factors, land and labour on the other hand. Such one-sided substitution makes the position of capital prominent and includes new types of capitalization and massive irrigation. Mechanization makes possible even substitution among different forms of capital. Animal power is substituted by machines as is substitution between labour and machines. The process of substitution being massive, capital emerges as an important input.

9

Financing Agriculture

Regarding finance, agriculture has many drawbacks that lead to under financing and consequently slow-down of the process of modernization. Efforts have been made in the form of varying experiments. They had limited success in the past. The traditional sources still operate, but they act against the interest of modernisation of agriculture.

It is prominently evident to all those who examine the problem of financing agriculture that the main source of finance in agriculture is the producer him/her self. The resources with them are extremely small, sometimes even not sufficient to meet the current expenses. This drawback is the major hurdle for development of agriculture.

We can compare and contrast the financing possibilities in agriculture with organised sector. In the organized sectors, the base is equity capital. Equity capital is mobilized on the basis of the project or plan for production and the plan gets acceptance partly on the basis of economic analysis which examines financial and technical feasibility. The economic feasibility depends on technical feasibility. The integrity of persons at the helm of affairs lends feasibility and integrity. People subscribe to the equity capital in the capital or investment market and the business unit gets started. Investment is drawn from the savings of two types, individual and corporation, even insurance companies, provident funds, etc. On the whole the organized sector basically initiates investment funds out of savings in the nation.

For agriculture, own savings are the primary source for investment in capital. Banks do extend loans but the amount is small and has severe conditions for repayment. Cooperatives were organized during the first quarter of twentieth century. These cooperative societies had severe conditions for repayment. The land was the basis for some years in the first quarter of twentieth century. The conditions were liberalized thereafter. Societies were allowed to have limited liability organization. The experience was sad. The loans were overdue in most cases and in few cases, the societies had to be wound up.

The period after planning was initiated and has seen liberal conditions. These were allowed to run in favour of indebted cultivators. Debts were legally allowed to be written off. New debts then would be very difficult. Banks were brought in after nationalization of banks. They were made to give loans to agriculture as prescribed portion of total loans. Since banks had limited outlet for rural areas RRB's (Regional Rural Banks) rural banks were opened in selected regions. They worked as rural branches of the scheduled banks. But, the experience was not happy. They had high cost of loan operations. The cooperative wing had an arm known as Land Mortgage Banks. They were expected to give loans mainly for assets purposes and were supposed to be for medium to long term. Medium term loans were extended for 5 years and long term loans were up to 20 years. The land mortgage banks did not make much progress. The main feature of cooperative sector was that the funds to operate were made available by the state to a large extent. The state too would not continue to write of the funds for infinite amount. Despite various drawbacks, cooperatives expanded with the state support. With banks entering the fray, the share of private sector like money lenders declined perceptibly. In the private lender sectors, relatives and acquaintances had a major share. Loans from relatives were convenient and less burdensome for these loans were without interest in most cases. But they were usually for short term like one season or one year.

Thus, the organized sector mainly in urban areas had an easy and extensive access to savings in the nation while agriculture had to depend largely on own savings which were meager. Various agencies that entered agriculture could give limited help. The slender source for tapping savings from the large section of urban areas through banking sector made more difficult to draw upon the major portion of national savings for agriculture.

As we observed, capital assets in agriculture required substantial investment. However, actual investment remained low till there was rapid increase in farm incomes.

Often it is pointed out that existence of tenancy and large number of small farmers further limited the investment in large capital. Small amounts of loans borrowed by farmers made loan transactions cost – heavy. In fact, the large scale investment as in the case of major irrigation schemes came from public sector. It was partly due to the nature of investment. The nature of investment required benefit to cover large areas and hence a large groups of individuals. The recovery of investment was partial and mainly through charges levied on the farmers who are potential users of irrigation. Even in this matter a distinction was made between those projects which were considered profit yielding and those which were of help to farmers. The former were given priority.

During the planning period, selection of irrigation projects was based on cost-benefit analysis. Both costs and benefits included not only direct but also indirect costs and benefits. Indirect costs were mainly displacement of farmers behind the dam and benefits included costs saved for averting draughts and famines. The former is likely to be under-estimated and the later could be over estimated.

Dams are likely to be silted up at a greater speed than usually estimated. Hence, the time taken for silting up is only an estimate and the actual period of active operation may deviate from the estimate. The difference can be a guess and deviation can be wider in reality. But underestimating of such indirect cost is likely at the time of planning.

The new sources of finance are always searched for. The microfinance is recent innovation. Mostly ladies are organized in a group for small trade and they jointly borrow. They jointly underwrite the responsibility for paying off the loan. The experiment is successful for payment of loan has been nearly 100 %. This has yet not been tried for agricultural investment on a large scale.

On the whole, the finance for agriculture is either limited and costly when the lending agency is personal like money lenders, or is rationed while public agencies like banks or cooperatives are involved. The self-finance therefore turns out to be the major source of investment, which by definition is limited for individual farmers. Hence, full potential of development is rarely realized. Negative investment which implies creating additional capital without addition to output is another source of reluctance for loan to farmers.

There is one more aspect of investment which should be mentioned at this stage. Investment in capital depends partly on the outlook of individual investor. If the loans are available with ease, those with optimistic outlook may over-borrow and fail to repay the loan. If the loan is from individual lender or from banks which have commitment to collect dues with some harsh measures, then the extreme results lead to suicides. So far this phenomenon has been limited, but it is like a tip of the iceberg reflecting the underlying harshness of borrowing activities.

There is one more hurdle which I should indicate. Research results accumulated over time or brought in from international platform seem to be brought to farmers. Green Revolution is the result of such activities. Yet farmers have little knowledge or experience. Despite this hurdle, the progress is rapid or seems so. For we know the operation of the learning curve. The risk takers jump in the fray at the outset. Their success prompts those who follow them. At the end come the laggards who trail in at the slow pace. This learning curve effect gives an apparent rapid progress. It takes time for others to follow. But the followers add to the pace of progress after which the progress tapers off. But if research activity is rich in results, then the progress will seem to continue. While the learning curve effect of the first widely accepted research is in operation, the new research results begin to be accepted with faster pace for learning curve effect based on experience of the first research results use. Farmers with experience get easily familiar with the new one. We can give some instances. The hybrid corn was brought in to production system around mid-thirties of the twentieth century in USA. But it did not reach other countries, and certainly not to India. It had to wait for three to four decades. In between, the improved variety of wheat which found Mexico as its home reached India under the condition of severe scarcity of food grains before the Green Revolution. Under these circumstances, the entire machinery of the state put its force to work and within relatively short period, it reached the ground level on a vast scale. Punjab took the lead. The Mexican variety could not cater to the palate of Indian consumer, the research workers spent their energy to improve the taste element and improved wheat with much larger production potential. It became widely accepted. Experience with paddy was similar and it followed wheat after a short interval. Exploitation of better production potential boosted farmers' enthusiasm and income levels and that led to higher investment out of own savings. Punjab took the lead regarding both wheat and paddy. In this process, extension services like development blocks floated by the government played a prominent role. Thus, research with extension services have to play a joint role for success.

We have discussed varying hardships of borrowing for agriculture. Agriculture has no access to funds generating equity and has very limited access to funds in public sector like banks and yet during the period of transition from traditional agriculture to modernized agriculture it has to find finance to fund the investment. The result is halting progress in spreading of new seeds and modernization as such. When the progress is on the basis of accumulated research results, the apparent progress may be rapid, but it is still below the realizable potential. The learning curve effect also may further slow down the pace of modernization compared to the potential available.

Yet another field for agriculture to generate additional income is in animal husbandry. We discuss that in the following chapter.

10

Animal Husbandry

When settled agriculture emerged from hunting and gathering stage, along with it the allied field of domesticated animals seems to have emerged. Scriptures mention cow as a valuable asset because it provides a flow of income in the form of dairy products. Settled agriculture seems to have entered the next stage from pick axe to the use of plough for tilling[1]. Around that time there was lot of land uncultivated. Grass used to grow on what was a common property. It was realized that the milking capacity of a cow was substantially higher than required to bring up the calf. Milk then emerged as a commodity for use by consumer and dairy products produced from milk were used for transactions for consumers' needs. Even the princes ruling over rural areas collected the dairy product as a tax recovery. The mountain back provided free grass.

Dairy that emerged then at the time of Krishna, subsequently emerged as a business commodity. The grass land as a common property declined. The use of plough and common consumption of dairy products made possible to treat both as joint product.

The economics of dairy industry came to play an important role. Animal husbandry provided internal positive returns to scale. The male calves of cows came to be used as bullocks.

Young ones were castrated at young age so that the energy is stored and used for cultivation. The use of grass as fodder declined but the stalks of grains were used as feed and fodder. The energy required for cultivation thus became available almost for free. The special characteristic of cow was her ability to survive the heat of pre-monsoon summer in India.

Cows were reared alongside buffaloes as a dairy animal. Except the areas of heavy rainfall, the male calves of buffaloes in drought prone areas are allowed to die with no nutrition saved from mother's milk. They are given butter-milk on which they cannot survive for more than a week according to the local experience. The milk production of buffaloes exceeded that of cows at the stage of full availability of fodder and feed. Buffaloes therefore outstripped the economic advantage of cows as a source of milk production. This became prominently evident after the Five Year Plans were initiated.

Even the technical advantage of buffaloes over cows was not adequate to generate what has come to be known as White Revolution. While in Green Revolution, technology played a leading role, in White Revolution (Dairy Revolution)) the well organized institution for marketing played a dominant role. What has come to be known as AMUL (Anand Milk Union Limited) model paved the way for revolution. The model has three outstanding features. The producers enrolled as members holding shares in the newly created milk marketing cooperative. Secondly, members delivered milk to the cooperative for which collection centers were set up. Thirdly, the price paid against the delivery was based on quality measured in terms of fat content. The members were satisfied with this arrangement. They got as dividend in addition to the amount against their deliveries. The AMUL was a dynamic organization. It employed highly trained employees at the helm. They helped organize the cross-breeding programme which helped improve the breed of cattle and subsequently the milk production. Increased milk production per animal reduced the cost per unit of milk. It resulted in increased incomes of members who were mainly farmers in the area. The irrigation extension and expansion of milk production made farmers rich. This attracted attention of farmers in other regions and the milk marketing with improved production resulted in improving the rank of India in the world.

Thus, the increased internal rates of return and scientific marketing together with improved breed and feed (concentrates) consumption was the key to new revolution.

Cross breeding of cows improved economy of dairy output for cows but it was claimed that the new breed had deterioration of male energy level. Cows therefore played less important role in White Revolution. Rapid privatization of common property further led to deterioration. Cows are used to stroll and when cows are stall-fed the major metamorphosis undergoes a change. The ability to compete with buffaloes takes a back seat.

One major point for the dairy industry should be noted. In India cows still have a prime position, but declining. Bull used for reproduction would have an optimum ratio of 1 bull for 60 cows. We have this ratio. But bulls, otherwise not productive, are not taken good care and hence the quality of breed is not maintained. AMUL model has included in it the veterinary doctors who go round the villages and take care of health of animal. They have helped checking the spread of infectious disease like foot and mouth. Rinderpest is another infectious disease. Between the two, they used to take heavy toll of livestock. Prevention of these diseases have saved animals and hence the wealth and production of dairy industry. This has helped raise income and asset value of farm business. The expected age of cows was 10-12 years and average would work out to 6-8. The injecting into animal husbandry profit element has reduced in reality the average life of cows as dairy animals. The average age in foreign countries where meat industry has swelled is approximately 5.8 years. The reason for low average age can be traced to the fact that the optimum production of milk is around that age and production tapers off thereafter. The owners prefer to wean animals with low production and send them to slaughter house where they are still valued for meat. In India, since cows are valued for their piety they are maintained beyond the optimum age. How long this value-based profession will hold is hard to guess. But in the mean while, buffaloes may take over the position of pride and the value as live animal is less preferred for them. Cattle industry as a whole may be seen as declining.

We should note that the cost of maintaining livestock on dry fodder is much below the cost of maintaining them on costly feed in western countries. This low cost of maintaining animals has made possible for India to have prime position among nations of the world in producing milk. The economics of animal husbandry may change as the time goes by and values (non-monetary) as the base of the industry deteriorate. Position of buffaloes in the dairy production makes any projection in to future complex. For, cross-bred cows can compete with buffaloes with success.

End Note

1. Lord Krishna is associated with grazing and Balabhadra with plough for tilling.

11

Overall Observations

We are at the threshold of the history of agriculture. The beginning was as an activity mainly to maintain family, but the effort was a joint endeavor. The rural society was a unified community. This is now disappearing. Rapid progress has been made in recent decades regarding organizing the evolution of higher level of technology in the pipeline and making it accessible through extension and credit. The group activity and group feeling have been atomized with the individual emerging as the main decision maker for both production of wealth and supply of labour.

In this process of change, the presence of the state has been an agency affecting motivation and as supplier of some of the vital production resources. Initiatives in certain vital areas have moved to the area under the state domain. This includes structure of agriculture through ownership of land and its operation. Similar massive entry of state is observed in the field of irrigation. There are two distinct areas, irrigation under the ownership and operation, for individuals, and for irrigation as a source of production input as well as initiative for construction and delivery of dams, canals for irrigation water based on initiative of the state.

Efforts were made for a short period for collective (as well as cooperative) farming to make production as a joint effort. The experiment lasted for a while, for the individual production had the preference of operators. State then took the back seat regarding decision-making at the production level. The market emerged as the main force. The state still kept it under its control where and when the market operation led to results not acceptable to the community. The price-control and/or price support emerged as the main tool for keeping market under control for obtaining the desirable results. Rationing of food initially and subsidized prices for delivery of grains and sugar are out come of the state level decision making. To make it successful, the state needed a supply in their hands for which they undertook support price programme. The state offered profitable prices assured for purchases by the state. The storage programme became a part of price support programme. Thus, Indian agriculture ceased to be a purely individual market operated activity and now it is a mixed operation. On the whole, it has worked satisfactorily, mostly when the production is not in short supply.

The Model of Indian agriculture is thus complex. The state intervenes on humanistic ground. But the results are not to the liking of the state or the producers. We can take two examples. The abolition of Zamindari system was supposed to benefit the occupants who got the ownership rights. And it did to the large extent. But one unexpected disadvantage emerged for which the state was not prepared. In India and especially, in the southern states, tanks played a major role for irrigation. Tanks were constructed and maintained traditionally by the big Zamindars. Their incentive was based on rent in kind. When the tanks were maintained to utilize the full capacity, the benefit was shared by Zamindars as well. With abolition of Zamindari, incentive to maintain tanks disappeared and the tanks soon were in disrepair. The result was two fold. In the traditional agriculture, production declined, in modernized agriculture the benefit derived decelerated. The state has yet to evolve a structure by which the initiative for maintenance can be protected at the state level and benefit can be realized at the producer level.

State has initiative in major and some medium irrigation projects. Their construction has meant benefit to farmers using irrigation. The problem that has complicated the deriving of benefits as desired pertains to riparian rights. Water distribution system does not assure the distribution evenly to those located at the mouth of canal and those at the tail end. Those at the tail end are not sure about whether they will get enough water to irrigate their crops, while those close to the mouth of canal shift their cropping pattern in favour of water intensive crops like paddy and even sugar cane. Different states have tried different systems of water distribution. Maharashtra has opted for the system in which the village level distribution is in turn by different users. It is called *Varabandhi.* The system in Maharashtra seems to assure just benefit to all covered by the irrigation system.

Riparian rights are established legally but the systems of water distribution have been debased over a period of time for two reasons. The legal process is usually long drawn out. It is therefore time consuming. Besides, the action becomes a class action. It is difficult in rural areas to make people join hands together for uncertain end results through a legal procedure. Also, the system is not free from corruption which further dilutes the expected benefits. The less enduring farmers are hurt by corruption out of proportion.

Considering the fact that India has drought conditions over substantial area, irrigation has a major role to play in crop production. Despite the shortcomings just mentioned, the progress of irrigation can be considered noteworthy. The potential is nearly fully exploited in so far as minor irrigation is concerned. In some parts, in fact, minor irrigation is over exploited. Tube wells are the major source for minor irrigation. Bunds across small rivers and rivulets are another form of minor irrigation. Where water level is not very low, wells and oil engines or electric motors are yet another form of irrigation. The water distribution is in the hands of individual owners. In some parts, markets have developed for sale of water to farmers. They also benefit from minor irrigation.

The progress of medium and major irrigation is less but it is still continuing at a slow pace. Besides the short comings just mentioned, there is a general disapproval of major irrigation on humanitarian grounds and some technical aspects as well. Among technical aspect is the process of silting. Silting can be controlled by growing trees in the area behind the dam. But beyond that the land is not directly under the state control. There is a growing tendency for deforesting in these areas. Deforesting leads to increased silting.

As mentioned earlier, yet another method of irrigation is of constructing bunds across rivulets. Instead of one major bund, several small bunds are constructed. The probability of their being silted up is not very low but the silt can be removed easily and at low cost.

Micro irrigation has made a small entry. Drib and sprinkler irrigation are two forms of micro irrigation. Bunds and micro irrigation depend on local initiatives. Such initiatives can be taken with speed and proficiency. The very fact that innovations are tried with quick successions stands witness to the fact that importance if irrigation is fully realized at the farm level. More importantly benefits outrun the cost by a healthy margin.

State intervention is seen glaringly in ownership structure of land through redefining land rights. The success of these steps is mixed. The abolition of Zamindaris is claimed to be quite successful. Tenancy reform was wanting. In case of tenancy reform, instead of tenants getting the rights, the tenancy went underground. In some instances, the tenants were evicted and in the case of rent being paid in kind practice continued off the record. We can ascribe this not entirely to absence of willingness of ryots to honour the legal commitment but to a substantial extent the emerging pattern reflected the play of economic forces.

Research works have shown that the in-kind rent was observed to obtain in large cases for food grains. The conditions attached to the contract varied and in the case of crops under

Green Revolution which required fertilizers to be used, the cost sharing changed from half and half to less than half for tenant, for fertilizer cost was heavy. This is one example. The cash crops carried mostly the cash rent. And it was observed that the cash and share rents were not in effect varied as to be in favour of land lord or tenant. It varied, as we saw, under economic requirements.

With rush to urban centers especially of the well-to-do land lords, they converted the rent in kind to rent in cash and the rent was reduced if the owner opted for tenant paying all production costs except the land revenue.

Thus, the spread of variety of contracts for tenancy when practiced tended to reflect the economic land rent. Where the tenancy was practiced underground, the risk was entirely of the owner. He would lose ownership and would get rent which was much lower than the economic rent if the tenant took to court. Quite a few landlords sold their land and got out of the cultivation of land on their own account. Thus, the effect of the intervention was varied but in most cases it tended to be closer to economic rent. Traditionally, share-rent had a major element of assured labour supply which was necessary because labour requirement varied due to drought conditions. Where irrigation entered the production system, the rent was higher than that for dry crops. Once again the traditions reflected more of operation of economic forces than the monopolistic tendency.

Generally, when the change is voluntary, surprisingly the adherence to proposed change is widespread. This is illustrated by Bhoodan movement. The Gandhian influence was still fresh during the initial years of planning. Vinoba Bhave, disciple of Gandhiji, initiated the movement to do justice to have-nots. He appealed to haves that they may donate one-sixth of their holding to the common pool out of which the land may be redistributed to remove the poverty conditions at the low levels of land holding or landless families in the village. He preached this step for the alternative was, it seemed violent action on large scale by the afflicted class. The movement was successful in the sense that the land collected and redistributed by appeal was much larger than the land collected and redistributed through Government action of Zamindari abolition and Land Ceiling Act. Even this voluntary action suffered from a few shortcomings. Those who received land through redistribution were not regular farmers. They lacked the important implements like ploughs and bullocks to cultivate land. Their effort to obtain them on hire meant in many cases delay in cultivation and thus missing important part of the season. The voluntary movement despite success died down because of short comings, but those who got land and could manage to get needed implements and bullock power stayed in the business.

State intervention in the third area was in regard to crop prices. This is not special to India, many developed countries have programmes to subsidize incomes. Price is determined by economic forces as they operate in the market. The economic prices in rural areas are results of short term supply and demand forces. If the futures markets are in operation, this drawback can be partially corrected. But no decision-making arrangement seems to emerge in the context of very long term consideration. The reason lies in the very characteristics of agriculture.

We are familiar with risk and uncertainties. In agriculture both obtain. Variations which can be measured in terms of std (Standard Deviation) can be overcome through risk management. But other disturbances which are more or less random or otherwise unpredictable create disturbances which cannot be easily overcome. If the disturbances are predictable, measures can be devised to over-come these disturbances. Even rainfall pattern does not easily yield to predictable pattern. However, measures like crop insurance are devised. Crop insurance is devised for the group or the area covered and not for individual holding.

Beside the weather, two major uncertainties are innovations and state interventions. Innovations are initiated at research management level. It has relation to the problems facing crop production. But results are not predictable. Revolutions in technology are beyond efforts of individual research scholars. Cross-breeding is one example. When there is a long period between two major researches, the production levels cannot be easily predicted during the intervening period even if the nature of researches are known and adoption of results when available are preplanned. The state interventions are with good motives but their implementations develop loop-holes. These loop-holes are not predictable.

Are these disturbances unique to agriculture? They are unique to agriculture in some respects. The innovations in industries may not be predictable. The IT revolution in recent times is one such example. But its spread is less unpredictable. In the past, industries have seen similar revolutions, one such being steam engine. Shipping, railways, auto industry and aviation in transport and electricity in energy generation are examples of industrial revolutions. They were not predictable, but their spread once the main finding was in place was less unpredictable. For the decision-makers involved in their spread are relatively few and resources they can muster are piped through existing institutions. Compared to industries, in agriculture decision makers are in millions and the institutes like credit and marketing are not in place for instant availability.

The vast difference between industries (including services) and agriculture regarding the risks involved makes agriculture go slow about the change desired. As a result, even during the normal times there is a major difference in annual growth rate between agriculture and industries. The state intervention has not succeeded in bridging the gap. Agriculture has therefore remained behind.

One distinct characteristic which affects particularly agriculture is not mentioned so far. It pertains to global warming. The reason is that global warming is not yet conclusively proved nor is universally accepted. Due to this debatable position of the phenomenon, I have not pursued its effect. Only briefly, shall indicate it here. If there is warming or rise in temperature, the end result could be increased frequency and severity of droughts and probably of famines. Can this be faced successfully? The answer is uncertain. It is this phenomenon which makes future prospects for agriculture less certain.

12

Agriculture Hereafter: Humane Solutions

We have laid down all possible aspects of agriculture. We have pointed out how economic forces play role. We have to project into the future the shape agriculture would and could take. We shall underplay the role of State intervention mainly for our understanding.

Two Economic factors can play a full-blown role. On production side the supply. Supply would be governed by production function on one hand and prices on the other. Production function is moulded by technological change which may be distantly influenced by prices. As we have seen, the technological changes will affect the inter- sectoral relationships. Technology that permits increased use of fertilizers or tractors or both would change the role of inputs used by agriculture. The change will be caused by factors brought in from non-agricultural sectors. The increased demand for inputs in agriculture flowing from non-agricultural sectors could mean increased supply from non-agricultural sectors and may be at increased prices. This happens in short term. In the medium or long term, the relationship between agriculture and non-agricultural sectors may tend to change. It would imply that the changed supply of inputs has increased elasticity. This increased elasticity may encourage increased use of non-agricultural inputs. Part of the increased supply elasticity for non-agricultural inputs may be passed on to supply of agricultural output and hence the marketed surplus (supply). Supply is usually inelastic, so also demand. As a result, relatively small changes in supply or demand result into large changes in prices. As we have discussed earlier, change in overall supply in agricultural output, especially food grains, enlarges out of proportion the changes in marketed supply. Thus, there is one more factor affecting the market supply. In this complicated picture, if we add supply influence due to the change caused by technology of production of non-agricultural inputs, the price fluctuations would emerge as a major phenomenon. It is this phenomenon which has scared even the developed economies and led them to resort to subsidies. Subsidies reduce the sharpness of the troughs and peaks in prices otherwise not manageable.

Compared to the need for increased supply of agricultural production including food grains, the wide oscillations of prices would make food grain markets unpredictable at least in the short term. And in the long term the price fluctuations are beyond the capacity to forecast confidently.

Thus, dealing with the economic forces affecting agriculture and its characteristics we find the emerging picture to be worrisome. Especially in the developing economies, the concern would be deeper compared to that in the developed economies. In developed economies, the share of agriculture in GDP and in workforce is low and thus manageable when needed. The cost of such corrective action will be less in developed economies. Even the financial burden of subsidies is bearable. In developing economies, the large share of work force employed in agriculture in the total work force compared to share of agriculture in GDP taking up any scheme that can substantially help agriculture would add relatively large burden on the economy as a whole. Taking up small schemes with State aid would be less effective. And here is the trap for agriculture in developing economies. Allowing agriculture to go through the transition with inhuman consequences is unacceptable to the democratic frame.

Is there a solution? The solution cannot be two pronged: raising income to match with the urban incomes which are higher and are rising faster compared to that in agriculture and along with it, assure full employment. In this chapter, I deal with solutions based on human values, to conclude our discussion on the fundamentals of Agricultural Economics.

Traditional agriculture was transformed into modern agriculture, and the latter has a room for the play of economic forces. But we learnt that the end result was not humane. Especially for a developing economy, the transition to the desired status of agriculture becoming a small part of the national economy is painful and any short cut may inflict further pain.

The traditional agriculture has built into it factor complementarities and the help it gets from technological change would inject an element of increased factor substitution.

The resulting major problems are two: (1) low income and (2) slow expansion of employment for now when the population and hence work force is expanding in rural areas. We should then accept that solution of either, and allow the other problem to take its solution.

We should accept also the fact that there is a fundamental difference between the rural and an urban community. Rural community is basically a social entity and hence permits group living. Neighbours live in neighbourhood. Individual families are familiar members of the community and they live in and around a given village. In urban areas and especially in metro cities, the individual has a weak bondage with others in the city. The individuals are bonded together through activities like organisation of work at work place, civil activities like clubs and religious institutions like Church or Temple or Mosque. We do not want to pursue the characteristics of rural and urban society further. But for our purpose what is important is that the root of the bondage is important. A village in rural areas is made of individuals and families that exist there for generations.

They have a sort of human relationship. On occasions like festivals they come together. On social events like wedding and death in a family, individuals come together with a sense of personal feelings. This feeling of belonging or common bondage helps economic activities too. Worker-employer relationship is a lasting relationship if not continuing forever. Employer would help workers in times of workers' needs. As J.R. Hicks has pointed out that wages in U.K. are not entirely economic phenomenon and hence workers are continued to be employed in work even when the demand for labour goes down temporarily. In return, the workers standby the employer when the demand once again returns to its normal level. This observation was based on the war time experiences. We can draw a comparable observation for rural areas in India. The caste system in India is an additional factor to recon with. It leads to stronger bondage within the caste but weak bondage between the castes. But this factor too did not make the economic bondage with social bondage any weaker.

We do not suggest that the social element in rural areas is not subject to wearing as the time passes. The influence of modernization and technological advance followed by incomes advancing unevenly has eroded the human element in mutual relations among classes. The influence is yet limited.

Considering the existence of social element, Gandhiji advanced the cause of Khadi and Swadeshi. The off-season leisure interpreted as unemployment attracted attention. Khadi programme was intended to attack seasonal rural unemployment. It was effective since the Lancashire and Manchester, the two leading textile centers of U.K. suffered in employment for export of textile to India declined. The power of hand-made textile however lasted for a while. Come War and the appeal of unemployment weakened and demand for Khadi could not keep up for filling the off-season unemployment. More importantly, Khadi helped in generating rural employment but the wage could not match with the inflation in prices. Currently, Khadi wearers are confined to a large extent to political personalities for whom it has become attire for uniform. The

Government has preferred to moot programmes like EGS (employment guarantee scheme). Swadeshi like Khadi helped the rural handicraft. But it had less appeal and less demand.

The third programme promoted by Gandhian thinking was trusteeship. It accepted that the income earned would be unequal, but those helping generating income can operate as trustees. The trustees will have income out of proportion but they will spend it for the benefit of the society as trustees. Thus unequal income levels will not result in unequal consumption, and thus protect the poor from suffering from penury.

The main features of Gandhian schemes were the initiative from voluntary agencies, and execution depended on individual family. Khadi was an extension of textile operation in pre-textile industry period. During pre-textile industry period spinning was done by house wives as a group of neighbours and weaving was done by village craftsmen, the local weavers, who worked with handlooms. The product was mainly for the family. Coloured cloth was produced by city dwelling dyers. The quality varied as required. There were specialists who made wedding saris at a high cost. The proverbial Patolas from Patan (Gujarat) were made by those who practiced the craft for generations. Cities like Ahmedabad thrived on textiles even before the textile industry established itself in the city. Small cities like Surat prospered with power loom when the textile industry in Ahmedabad declined. Textile industries devoted to specialized products in cities like Dharmavaram in Andhra Pradesh and Coimbatore in Tamil Nadu still have the traces of the link with the past. Dharmavaram produces silk textiles. Traditional centers known for their craftsmanship are Banaras (now known as Varanasi), Jaipur (known for *Bandhani* (tie and dye design). On the whole, the traditional textile and the modern textile industry both are on decline. They cannot play any role in solving the problems of rural areas unless a new approach is discovered.

We have to dig deep to get the ultimate solution to the problem of economic well being or what is known as economic welfare. It is convenient to separate economic welfare and general happiness. But keeping them separate all the time and all the while prevents reaching the solution to overall happiness.

For economic well beings, the solution commonly suggested for rural improvement is speedy urbanisation. We have looked into it and we find the intervening period when transition from dominance of rural to dominance of urban areas will be grueling for those involved in it either by moving out or accepting the present situation they are in, in rural areas as beyond solution. Institutions like credit or marketing have an upper hand and the participants feel they are helpless. We have seen the same feeling, the feeling of helplessness pervades regarding the weather behaviour.

The probable solution which cannot cure inequality but make it tolerable is of infusing human values for shaping the public behaviour of private individuals. The relatively richer individuals may have a charitable outlook for using their high incomes. They would look at residents in a village as members of one family and see to it that *no one goes to bed on empty stomach.* The surplus they have earned in any given year is made possible by the joint effort of all members of the society as a whole. All residents have the same Lord (God) in them and any misery that makes any resident suffer means suffering for all residents who are but the progeny of the same Lord. The ultimate truth would make them imbibe this spirit of oneness among the residents. Thus, despite the unequal incomes the members of the village would feel the spirit of belonging to the common group of people. Unequal incomes may be partly due to some social factors and some economic factors. A widow with young children and herself (the only adult) as an earning member of the family may try to work hard; even then she cannot reach the level of average income for families in the village. Even she may barely maintain family with enough to eat and dress and have decent roof over head. Similarly, migration of young ones to urban areas to earn barely minimum, leaving behind aged parents or grandparents will find that their elders live in poverty and helplessness. Recently this was discovered by members of a voluntary organisation in Tamil Nadu that the village they visited had a lady suffering from paralysis and totally helpless going without meals unless someone takes care of her. Her situation changed when the volunteers agreed to help her in turn.

What is happening as isolated events should show up as a given phenomenon flowing from the inner hearts as a product of love. Such love can cure other ills and general level of happiness may improve. Can we wait for this to happen? We have a choice to make. We walk the economic way, which too cannot bring in equality to the general satisfaction, or we practice from children up to elders the love for human beings to minimize the suffering. Not easy but probable. We should make it possible by evolving appropriate institutions with committed participants.

We have to scratch the fundamentals here. Both agricultural and nonagricultural production activities operate on two basic dimensions. They are, time and space. Agriculture has lot more to do with space in the form of area of land used as an input. It can hardly be compressed. For nonagricultural production activities, time is an important input. If time involved can be compressed, meaning for given time more output is obtained, then the efficiency is improved and incomes rise. This is the process known as labour (time) substitution by other (mainly capital) inputs. Since less labour is required with compression of time, the production activity comes to be centralized in space. A few workers require less area for their stay and work.

In agriculture, weather makes it less convenient to compress time through labour substitution, unless the space is also compressed. Compressing space here would mean, for given land more is produced. Consequently, per worker area of land used is reduced. Small holdings replace large area of dry farming. But per worker output is not reduced so substantially that the workers can work in a concentrated area as in the case of nonagricultural production where activities are concentrated in urban centers.

Yet another example is worth examining. It was assumed that emergence of electricity as an input would make decentralized production activities plausible. It did not happen. Supervision required for technically advanced processes did not allow decentralized production on a large scale. Similarly in agriculture, centralized production did not succeed. Production activities are still spread over vast area. Labour time is compressed for production through mechanization of certain processes like cultivation, harvesting, transplanting and even transporting.

These two distinctly different basic characteristics of agriculture and nonagriculture lead to distinctly different organisations. Corporations established in big cities provided the main hub of production activities for industries and services like energy production. Agriculture remained basically individual-producer based activity around villages.

The above differences have continued to plague the organization of production activities in the three sectors (including the service sector). The services sectors like health care and education follow the concentration of people. Urban centers therefore have concentration of health care and of reputed education centers with even research facilities.

We have to search for solution of the current problems of rural areas within the frame work we are given by the basic characteristics. Especially we have to have suitable organization of production, storage and health care and education activities vastly decentralized. Since workers are located in basically decentralized locations in rural areas, we have to provide there suitable storage facilities for producers. The first institution here could be one in which small number of producers come together for storage of harvest to carry it over to nonharvest season or even to the following year(s). The micro credit organization now in operation immediately appeals for it. The finance can be obtained from the credit organization first, for the construction of storage facility and then for holding the surplus harvest under the individual title to the stored material. The organization which would take care of bringing the members together would also help bringing activities involved also together. Surplus in harvest can be converted into savings from income. In the event of drought or famine the grain required can be taken out from the surplus of the preceding years if available, if not, purchase may be arranged from local residents or from outside as found necessary and convenient. Credit will be involved at this stage for which joint binding may serve as the basis.

The weather may play a random factor role. Also, random factor may be illness of an earning member that strikes the family and makes the members to borrow under stressful conditions. If it happens for a few families in the village and they have nowhere to turn to, the relatively well to do with some surplus with them can help. Presently, this practice takes the form of convenience loans or regular loans carrying interest. In the reform we are aiming at, it can be a part of joint operation. But if the misery is not random and temporary, the solution has to be sought in finding new and lasting help. We have examined the reasons for such eventuality. The currently accepted solution supported by the Government is EGS (employment guaranteed scheme). Alternative solution that may fit into the basic characteristic of agriculture of decentralized production could be suggested here. The storage activity groups may be organized, or if possible the same group can undertake multiple activities and include production activity other than agriculture. A small area may be allotted to this activity. Since next to food, clothing is the basic requirement, spinning followed by weaving may be undertaken. This may be preceded by sliver making. Small machine like Ambar Charkhas may be made available to the needy. The family may add directly to their income without going to distant places and undertaking back-breaking activities. Spinning could be one such activity which may target the need of the family directly and thus help relieve part of the poverty. It may lead to 10 % addition to income. Art work based on knitting is yet another activity that will meet the criterion of decentralized activity close to home. In the village, there might be craftsmen and they may be organized around their crafts. In any case, there will be need for organizing marketing of crops and other products produced to raise incomes and to remove poverty. This will not prevent out-migration but such organization would make it humane. Out migration would be by preference of the family or the individuals. Those with higher education level may be most willing to search for suitable jobs outside the village, mostly in cities.

The successful organisation around safe and secure supply of food grain at village level would make it easy to organize other production activities and activities like health care and education. Every year, a number of teachers retire from service. Their services may be useful for organizing education activities nearer home in the village or around it. For health care, similar organisation may be evolved which can handle some common ailments. Complemented by availability of safe and secure drinking water, sanitary facility would make living in villages a little more acceptable and less outrageous than it is today.

While these activities are available in some form, the point I am making is that they will be made within easy reach of most, if not all. When these organizations find their foothold, one can say the general atmosphere in villages would add to overall happiness. The standard of life will be better than it could be by merely raising general income levels. Those living in these villages will find that their respect for human values for the group as a whole would be better even than that in urban cities. After all, life is for total happiness of all concerned and not for enjoying material wealth and that too for relatively few.

Appendix - I

Human and Social Capital

We discussed in the preceding chapters physical capital. Accumulation is in response to economic stimuli. Will the same stimuli lead to accumulation of human capital? Before we answer this question we have to acquaint, with ourselves human capital. The term evolved and came into common use in fifties of last century. Prof. T.W. Schultz of Chicago University gave this term to the profession. According to him, education is the prime human capital. When a child or even an adult has an opportunity to get acquainted with written words and figures, a whole new world opens before him her. Till now he/she was familiar with the outside world only with sense organs like eyes, ears and sense of touch. Certainly people could manipulate this information for personal use which included practicing agriculture. A fine sense of benefiting from the direct knowledge people could accumulate, led them to follow the profession and traditional practices developed. There was slow but sure addition to the existing knowledge, but it was slow and the growth that followed mostly helped to sustain or marginally improve the living condition. With formal education, the process changed radically. Prof. Schultz demonstrated that introducing primary or elementary education yielded returns which outstripped returns on physical capital. Following the same argument in recent literature it has been shown that higher education gives better return over the primary education.

The above propositions can be extended and it can be shown that at any point in time, enhanced education adds to the enlightenment in the society and thus adds to the capacity of the society to generate the growth of the economy at a rapid pace. This general statement is valid for rural and urban areas and within rural areas for agriculture as well.

But the problem gets a twist when those with education look for employment outside rural areas. Their migration to urban areas creates a trough in the rural areas and the human capital accumulation gets a setback to this extent till the rural area generates dynamic forces for the rapid growth of education level so as to cope up with the growing demand for education in urban areas and also within rural areas. This becomes an enigma, especially in developing economies. They as such begin the new process of accumulating human capital at a fairly rapid rate. There, the low capacity to expand the knowledge acts as a constraint rather than leading to periodic stimuli. Dynamic development of education in rural areas need a quantum jump in education in rural areas in developing economies and for successful measure will lead to the entry of the state and a plea for compulsory and free primary and even sometime secondary education. Once this happens and there is an encouraging response from the benefitted recipients, advanced level education gets a boost. Especially, the elite from the urban areas and those from rural areas who constitute the upper middle class like big owners of land, show a special liking for urban environment, especially of education.

Thus we see economic forces taking over and generating the rapid process of quantum jump in human capital. The state does not take the backseat but confines itself to acting as an agent to help the process rather than generate the process and take a lead as it has the role of leadership for primary education and some time even in the higher education. What happens then is rapid expansion of the base level of education in rural areas and upper level education expansion in urban areas, the former in the public sector and the latter in the private sector. When education at the base level is universal and hence returns to it stabilize at the natural level with incentive for it remaining constant, its glamour is nearly vanished. The result is that the link between the growth and primary education becomes slim.

At present, the State is confining its pivotal role to the base. This leads to the limited facility for higher level education, it being below the level of demand for it. In the market place, the forces so act that the urban areas are the primary beneficiary and secondly the regulation of quality is underplayed. What has come to be known as donations for getting a seat reflecting higher price which only a few can afford. Donations for seats in special education would reduce the emphasis on quality education. Politically, the emphasis shifts to reservations for lower classes which are also in minority. This may be justifiable for taking special care of minorities but may not justify from the point of quality education. Thus the picture of education becomes lopsided. It has however served one purpose, the current boom in the service sector and especially IT sector is helped. The country as a whole benefits, though not evenly. The trickle effect of IT revolution especially to rural areas is miniscule.

Human capital includes health, beside education. Better health means improved efficiency level at work, both in urban and rural areas. Better health depends on better medical facilities to ward off diseases and better nutrition for better ability to work and to prevent diseases. Medical science has made robust progress, but it is difficult to carry it to rural areas and especially remote areas. This disability is shared with the education which is discussed above. Better nutrition depends on better awareness and affordability. Rural areas lack both.

We have so far confined our observations to identifiable forms and measurable quantity of human capital. They have an advantage for immediate results or results that are quantifiable. But we should remember that just as individuals have their identity, so also society has its identity. Hence it is said that education is for life and not for living. Living is measurable in terms of income per head or wealth for the family. If we accept these standards we shall be in the trap of 'more and more' of the wealth for individuals. For poor countries this is a far off issue, but for the rich countries this is the present day problem. Water and energy use provide the instances. Against the general water scarcity per head per day, water use in USA is about 80 gallons. If India pursues USA level the ghost of water scarcity will hound here with increased ferocity.

In a society, if such values as truthfulness, compassion, love for fellow beings and peace are practiced, the general welfare would rise and reach a high level. The haves would take care of fellow beings to see no one goes to bed on an empty stomach. We have two situations, one, the incomes are rising, but at the lower end , there are still families which have to miss a meal and their conditions will not improve visibly in near future; and two, the incomes rise but those who have higher incomes share their wealth with love and compassion with less fortunate. Less fortunate may be those whom the nature has dealt with a mortal blow like widows. The society that has an accepted standard of love and compassion and has evolved organisations that can be a conduit for human welfare can be said to have higher social capital in the form of social welfare. And hence, it has higher social capital. Here we define conducive behaviour in the society as social capital. Normally, social capital includes mainly infrastructure like transport, energy, railways, even rivers and mountains, forests and coastlines are included in social capital for they help the society as a whole to grow. We had a plan once and it may still be on records to link rivers north-south to improve the transport link. All these are social capital. But we have now reached a stage when peaceful and helpful behaviour should be included in social capital. Its outcome can be measured in terms of improved conditions of the lower sections of the society and where possible help can be rendered by the upper class.

Some of the problems witnessed in today's world include people going to bed without meal, and high crime rates. Terrorism, dissatisfaction of people with the existing conditions and their protest against them are extreme forms of negative social capital. When that is reduced, we can have increased social capital.

Should we have two types of social capital kept separate and measured uniquely? The physical social capital mostly infrastructure may be kept separate. The behavioural capital may be kept similarly separate. We have examples of measuring standard of living and it includes now education level, death rates, and infant mortality rates as part of standard of living.

We shall leave the issue here. But we shall remember that the issue has to be attended to.

As far as the exercise of production function is concerned, we shall accept that the large part of human capital and now even social capital remain hidden as a part of the remainder, the unexplained part of the production related to inputs.

Appendix - II

Village Level Organisation – A Model

Each village is a sort of social unit, a neighbourhood above family unit. In between, groups along caste line play a distinct role. Social unit of neighbourhood is identifiable but is amorphous. We make an attempt here for delineating a specific organisation that will deal with the major issues at village level. It would involve handling money and marketing but not directly with banking. I now lay down the out line.

A word of caution at this stage is in place. This is not an attempt to obliterate a link that is emerging between villages and urban areas. Accounts of such link provide the picture which is not pleasant. Here is an attempt to make the link more humane.

The proposed organisation will not be a part of Village Panchayat which has its own legal identity and political form based on voting.

Village life has three aspects that need better organisation with dedicated efforts. Panchayats take care of sanitation and road links within the village and a guest house and a meeting place like Panchayat Ghar and most importantly houses village records for population and land use, land ownership and tenancy rights and irrigation. The organisation we propose goes beyond this.

The three aspects we mentioned have include management of harvest, employment generation leading to full employment and to the extent possible organize activities around the objective of increased income levels through increased earnings. We take them up below seriatim.

In economics, we emphasize decision making and for most part it rests on individuals, whether it is about production or selling what is produced, raising income or saving a part of it and invest it in the pursuit of income generation. In the case of individuals who work for others, the field of decision making for individuals becomes limited. In all these cases for wage earners, the effect of individual decision is marginal.

Society is made up of individuals and if they take joint decisions their decision is not lost in the vast ocean. Individuals do not remain nonentity especially when the decision pertains to consumption in addition to decision regarding production. Here comes the role of reforms of the economic organisation we are about to propose.

We propose that at village level an agency may be organized for handling one function, viz. storage. But there is one difference. We allow the individual producer to choose the price level he/she wants based on market dependency. The price may vary according to the timing and market agency chosen. The agency we suggest makes a link between consumption and producer as is the case of individual if he/she takes up the function of storage.

Let us name the agency. It may be called Village Trust VT. It will not be registered under Law of Cooperatives. The difference lies in one major condition. VT undertakes to sell back to the individual producer, the kind of produce sold to VT earlier in the year by the producer, may be at the harvest time. The individual producer will avail of the facility to buy back, maybe during off season at the price at which he had earlier sold his produce plus the cost of storage and handling. The whole idea is that multiple agencies that we presently have may be reduced and hence profits they earn would disappear. The major advantage of this arrangement is that at the off season time when prices are much higher, the producer will get as if his own produce back at the price he had earned. This will be great relief. This is not without a cost. We are transferring the function of storage and marketing in driblets to the new organization (VT) without the producer losing the control. There might be problems in allowing the functioning of VT successfully. But we trust that the local talent with local goodwill can solve these problems.

In case, the producer does not want to buy back and VT decides to sell in the market at higher price and thus earn profit, the profit will be returned to the individual member. (Members will jointly decide about the mode of calculating profit and also the amount of produce to be carried over to the future so that in case the following year is drought year, the member retains the right to buy back with the price he had earned when he sold. We would observe that VT differs from cooperative marketing society that had been tried and still has been under operation. Cooperative marketing society did not spread widely. If at all, VT would have some resemblance to Self Help Groups.

The arrangement covers the risk of drought years when otherwise the producer is required to buy from the market at the current prices which are much higher. There are two risks: one, of off-season risk within the year, and two, drought year risk. These are targeted to bring life to economic life in the village.

We do see here the need for finance required for transactions of buying initially and also for creating storage facility. Bank loan under government guarantee can be one way. We claim that this arrangement will benefit the village as a whole. Labour can join the VT if they have an option to have wages in kind. Out of wages earned, if they have surplus early on, they can use VT for storage facilities. Other conditions would apply to the members to have an option to have special conditions for labour to aid them have relief, if required.

Second objective of VT is generating employment in case a section of residents need during the off-season. Since VT is a local organisation, those managing it would know the employment situation and also the need for labour for common village programmes and also for private work. The common programmes may include transport links to the nearest regular road or bus stop or railway station. We need not go into the details that the management can well handle. One programme that we can suggest pertains to making the harvest-preservation ready. Additionally, the handling of the stored material as the need arises for distribution for the buy-back programme. If there is cultivable waste land in the village, it can be used for cultivation of vegetables and herbs for common illnesses where possible. Many such imaginative programmes can be taken up through group action. The approach here is: 'what is not possible by individuals is possible by group action'. If local good-will is yoked to the programme the work may have rich results.

Beside the labour employment projects, there may be, opportunity for production activities for private needs. Amber Charkha can be deployed in a central place where those in need can work and produce yarn which can be taken to weavers near by and thus have the clothes for the family. This may be a marginal activity for some villages, but for others it may be means to add to income for attaining decent living. The enterprising management can conceive village handicraft involving artistic skill for which markets are expanding. Such activities can bring robust earnings to BPL families.

This takes us to the third objective, viz. raising incomes. Additional incomes can be generated in the main occupation, which in this case is agriculture.

The research in agriculture is a continuous activity. At the local level, extension agency can be the link for facilitating adoption of what is new, suitable, tried and promising. VT can help the enterprising farmers with making available the raw material required and the finance involved for the production of crops. We are familiar with the untoward instances of farmer suicides. Caution and knowledge will stand in good stead for these programmes.

On the whole, VT may work in association with the field level agencies and in their cooperation. Each step is a venture and the village elders, if knowledge and experience are their forte, can be of valuable help.

While other programmes of the state are in the field, VT can provide a conduit for development and better efficiency.

Appendix III

Statistical Tables

Table - I : Land Use Changes (1) British India

[Million Hectare]

	Reported Area	*Forest*	*Available for cultivation*	*Cultivable Waste*	*Current Fallow*	*Net Sown Area*	*Cultivated area (Col +Col 6)*
1901-02	182.01	22.33	33.66	38.73	16.06	76.20	92.88
%	(100.00)	(12.03)	(18.05)	(20.57)	(8.81)	(41.08)	(50.7)
1911-12	205.31	25.04	42.20	35.95	20.17	82.01	102.12
1921-22	205.52	21.18	39.58	36.48	18.98	85.84	102.72
1931-32	206.80	26.78	39.58	38.49	18.17	85.59	103.67
1941-42	207.25	27.87	35.86	37.32	19.08	86.32	105.40
%	(100.00)	(12.38)	(17.08)	(18.09)	(14.07)	(40.02)	(56.53)
Growth Rate GPA	(0.32)	(0.54)	(0.23)	(0.25)	(0.43)	(0.31)	(0.33)

Contd.

(Contd.Table - I)

	Reported Area	*Forest*	*Available for cultivation*	*Cultivable Waste*	*Current Fallow*	*Net Sown Area*	*Cultivated area (Col +Col 6)*
1951-52	287.80	48.89	50.17	40.40	28.96	119.40	148.80
%	(100.00)	(17.01)	(17.54)	(14.00)	(10.12)	(40.25).	(50.51)
1961-62	305.35	60.84	50.31	36.50	25.23	136.40	157.37
1971-72	306.62	65.41	41.62	34.66	24.53	137.58	162.11
1981-82	304.11	67.35	39.95	31.85	24.17	137.59	161.76
1991-92	304.84	67.98	40.91	29.40	23.93	142.72	166.55
2001.02	305.1	79.81	41.78	27.36	141.52	166.36	24.95
%	(100.00)	(22.89)	(13.10)	(9.08)	(46.04)	(50.04)	(8.12)
GPA	(0.12)	(0.70)	(-0.39)	(-0.78)	(0.38)	(0.23)	(-0.30)

GPA = Growth rate per annum.

Source:- Land use Change and Agricultural Growth in India (Pakistan and Bangladesh) 1901 to 2003, by Takashi Kurosaki, November 2007, Institute of Economic Research Hitotsubashi University, Tokyo, Japan Same source for table I and II *** 1%** 5% 8 10% Probability of statistically acceptable.

Note on table I: Total reported area varied within small margin. For land was recorded approximately in Zamindari areas and Princes States. The expansion of cultivated area is also marginal a little more than the increase in Reported area. In independent India the land seems to have been moved from cultivable waste and current fallow over a long period of time and that too is marginal. The observation that emerges is that extensive cultivation has reached a limit.

Table - II : Output value

Year	*Output value (Total)*		*Output Value per Capita*		*Value per acre*	
	Gr.Rate	*C.V.%*	*Gr.Rate*	*C.V.%*	*Gr.Rate*	*C.V.%*
1901-02 -10-11	1.31	11.6	0.16	11.6	-0.25	4.8
1911-12 – 20-21	-0.81	13.3	-8.0	13.3	-0.47	8.1
1921-22- 30-31	0.05	2.7	-7.6**	2.7	-0.28	2.5
1931-32 – 40-41	0.28	4.0	-1.11**	4.0	0.15	3.7
1941-42 -50-51	-.0.52	4.2	-7.6**	4.2	1.43**	4.0
1951-52-60-61	4.24***	5.1	-2.28**	5.7	2.34**	4.2
1961-62- 70-71	2.53**	8.8	-10.32***	8.8	1.89**	7.2
1971-72 – 8081	2.32***	7.1	-10.41	7.1	2.12***	5.6
1981-82- 90-91	3.23**	6.2	1.07	6.2	3.23***	3.7
1991-92-2000-01	1.68***	3.5	-.0.27	3.5	1.60***	2.8
19001-02-46-47	0.43***	8.7	-0.38***	10.0***	-0.04	6.2
1947-48 -2003-04	2.72***	7.5	0.60***	7.6***	2.19	6.8**

Note : Table II Output Value

There was nearly continued growth in total value except the World War I decade. Traditionally fluctuations from year to year were visible except post-World War I decade (1921-30) During inter -War years growth of total value shied of 1/2 per cent per year.

The growth in total value was not enough to give positive growth of per capita value despite the fact that population growth was mild around 1% per year except the first decade of the 20th century and the decade of eighties in last century the per capita value of output was in red. This was irrespective of the widely varyingt rates of growth of population. Population growth accelerated during the last two quarters of the past century. The dynamism in Indian agriculture is limited and did not last for decades. The intensive cultivation judged on the basis of per-acre value of production was in red during the first two decades of twentieth century it picked up in thirties and accelerated during the last half of the twentieth century.

Table 3 : Capital Formation in and For Agriculture

Rs Crores		*In 1993-94 Price*			
Year	*Gross Domestic Product*	*Gross Fixed Capital Formation*	*Gross Fixed Capital Formation*	*Percentage Shares*	*Percentage Shares*
		In	*For*	*In*	*For*
1980-81	401,128	15720	19299	3.4	4.3
1985-86	513,950	13061	17652	2.5	3.4
1990-91	692,871	15805	21560	2.3	3.1
1995-96	899,578	16824	25083	1.9	2.8
2000-91	1,198,625	18760	27946	1.5	2.3
2000-02	1,255,424	19880	28830	1.6	2.3

(Contd.)

(Contd. Table-3)

Year	*Rs Crores* *Gross Domestic Product*	*In 1993-94 Price* *Gross Fixed Capital Formation*	*Gross Fixed Capital Formation*	*Percentage Shares*	*Percentage Shares*
					[Public Sector
1980-81	401,128	7358	9855	1.8	2.1
1985-86	513,950	6005	9224	1.2	1.8
1990-91	692,871	4871	8706	0.7	1.3
1995-96	899,578	5318	9631	0.6	1.1
1999-00		4637	9902	0.4	0.9

Source: Report of the Committee on Capital Formation in agriculture.
Chairman: Bandopadhyay Director, Institute of Economic Growth, New Delhi 2003 Directorate of Economics and Statistics, Department of Agriculture and Cooperation Ministry of Agriculture Government of India.

Note Table 3: Capital formation in and for A 3 Capital Formation in and for Agriculture Between 1980 and 2000 the GDP increased at a simple rate of annual growth 0.156 while capital formation in agriculture grew at 0.064 and that for agriculture grew at 0.07 Ratio of Capital/output in agriculture hovered between 2 and 3. This will give the newly created capacity to be around 2%. barely sufficient to match the population growth.

Table 4 : Shift to Commercial Crops

Percentage shares to total cropped area 23	2002-03
Paddy	23.79
Wheat	14.06
Coarse Cereals	13.26
Total Cereals	15.38
Pulses	12.08
Total Food grains	65.70
Vegetables	2.96
Oil Seeds	13.54
Sugar Cane	2.70
Cotton	4.36

Source: as above.

***Note*:** Table 4 Commercialization The above data are very instructive. Commercial crops have limited area even after five decades of planning. Food grains still dominate. Indian Agriculture is entering phase of marketization with help of major food grains. Increased production now enters market leading to increased marketable-surplus.

Next important phase is of expansion of allied occupations like animal husbandry.

Details are given below :

Table 5 : Irrigation

	Percentage Irrigated Area:- Net and Gross	
Year	*Gross Irrigated Area as Percentage to Gross Cropped Area*	*Net Irrigated Area as Percentage to Net Cropped Area*
1950-51	22.51	20.35
1960-61	27.98	24.66
1970-71	38.15	31.86

(Contd.)

(Contd.Table 5)

Year	*Percentage Irrigated Area Net and Gross* — *Gross Irrigated Area as Percentage to Gross Cropped Area*	*Net Irrigated Area as Percentage to Net Cropped Area*
1980-81	49.76	38.76
1990-91	65.26	48.02
2000-01	77.98	54.62

Source: Department of Agriculture and Cooperation Ministry of Agriculture, Government of India.

***Note*:** Table 5 Irrigation : The explosive growth of irrigated area was made possible first by public sector investment followed by farmers' investment. The latter was in the form of minor irrigation through tube wells. Irrigation along with improved seeds and extensive use of fertilizers helped. This was mainly private adventure.

Table 6 : Livestock Population

(millions)

Category	*1951*	*1961*	*1971*	*1982*	*1992*
Cattle	150.30	177.60	178.30	192.50	204.60
Adult Female cattle	54.40	51.00	53.40	59.20	64.40
Buffalo	43.40	51.20	53.40	62.00	82.40
Adult Female buffalo	21.00	24.03	25.40	31.30	43.80

Source: As above.

***Note*:** Buffalo population nearly doubled, that of cow increased but much less. Target moved to efficiency rather than religion.

Table 7: Cereals and other Food Items

(Percentage Share in Expenditure on Food Consumption)

Year	*Rural*		*Urban*	
	Cereals	*Non-cereals*	*Cereals*	*Non-cereals*
1987-88	40.99	60.01	26.46	73.54
1993-94	38.30	61.70	25.69	74.31

(Contd.)

(Contd. Table 7)

Year	Rural		Urban	
	Cereals	Non-cereals	Cereals	Non-cereals
1999-2000	37.31	62.49	25.70	74.30
2001-02	34.55	65.45	24.30	75.70
2003	33.41	66.58	23.72	76.28

***Note*:** Non- cereals may be taken as quality food. Its share is increasing in both rural and urban areas. However increase is slow and minimal.

Table 8: Terms of Trade between Agriculture and Non-Agricultural Sectors

Base 1991 = 100

Year	Prices Received	Final Consumption	Prices Paid	Terms of Trade
1982-83	60.3	58.8	66.00	91.4
1990-91	112.3	112.1	110.2	101.9
2000-01	225	220.5	222.9	100.9
2004-05	260.1	251.3	252.5	100.7

Source: Department of Economics and Statistics, Ministry of Agriculture.

***Note*:** Terms of trade during the period of Green Revolution were not moving against agriculture though they did not move visibly in favor of agriculture too. For growth incentive came from technology.

Table 9: Share of Agriculture in GDP and in Employment

Year	Share of Agriculture in GDP 2000-01 prices	Share of Agriculture in Employment	Workers' Productivity ratio Agriculture /Non -agriculture	Workers' Productivity ratio Non-agriculture / Agriculture
1972-73	47.2	73.5	0.26	3.82
1983-84	30.2	63.7	0.24	4.12

(Contd.)

(Contd. Table 9)

Year	*Share of Agriculture in GDP 2000-01 prices*	*Share of Agriculture in Employment*	*Workers' Productivity ratio Agriculture / Non -agriculture*	*Workers' Productivity ratio Non-agriculture / Agriculture*
1999-00	25.1	60.4	0.22	4.55
2004-05	20.6	58.5	0.20	5.12

Source: Report of the Expert Group on Agriculture Indebtedness, Chairman Radhakrishna 2007, Quoted from CSO, National Accounts (Various Years).

Note: Trap for agriculture is evident. Share of agriculture in GDP declines at a faster rate than its share in employment leading to widening gap between productivity per worker in the agricultural and non-agricultural sectors. Instead of it being a motive to move to urban sector it adds to the burden of economic backwardness in agriculture relative to that in urban sector.

Table 10: Credit and Its Share in Input and Primary Sector in Total Credit

Year	*Short term credit as Percentage to Input Expenditure*	*Term Credit as Percentage of Primary Sector*	*Total Credit as Percentage of agriculture GDP*
1980-81	13.4	58.3	7.8
1985-86	15.3	73.0	8.0
1990-91	16.2	34.4	6.8
1996-97	22.2	55.7	7.7
1999-00	38.3	41.7	10.4
2004-05	51.1	81.0	25.1

Source: Expert Group on Agricultural Credit.

Note: During dynamic period of Green Revolution Credit started an increasing role. Yet till recently agricultural activity has remained mainly self finance.

Table 11: SHG linkage with Banks (Micro Credit)

Year	*SHG Financed by Banks (000)*	*Bank loans (Rs Crores)*
1992.93	53.00	51.07
2001-02	481.48	1018.54
2005-06	2255.87	11781.00

Source: As above.

Note **:** A new dimension of micro credit made revolutionary progress, a hope for future.

All together farmer households ventured for credit utilization with 48.8% had debt with average loan Rs 12555 per household. We should weigh before this opportunity for productive use of loan with Green Revolution technology and irrigation.

Table 12: Productive and Non-productive Loans –(percent)

	1961	*1971*	*1981*	*2002*
Productive	40.1	54.0	71.8	82.9
Non-productive	60.0	46.0	28.2	18.1

Source: As above.

Note: The structure of loan changed radically in four decades with productive use of loan dominating in the end.

Table 13: Credit Agencies

Agency	*1951*	*1961*	*1971*	*1981*	*1991*	*2002*
Institutions (Total)	7.5	18.7	31.7	63.2	86.3	81.1
Coops	3.3	2.8	22.5	26.8	30.0	35.2
Commercial Banks	0.8	0.8	7.4	25.8	35.2	28.3
Non-Institutional	96.7	81.3	66.3	35.8	13.8	18.8
Money lenders	88.3	48.7	30.1	16.1	17.8	16.8

Source: As above.

Note**:** The table amply demonstrates diminution of place of non-institutional agencies. They were replaced by cooperatives and commercial banks.

Table 14: Size of Land Holding and Credit - Institutional and Non-institutional

Size of Holding (ha)	*Incidence of Indebtedness*	*Institutional*	*Non-institutional*
<0.001	45.5	22.2	77.0
0.001 to 0.04	44.4	43.5	56.7
0.04 to 1.00	45.8	51.8	47.3
1.01 to 2.00	51.8	57.8	42.3
Up to 2.00	46.3	51.3	49.7
2.01 to 4.00	58.2	65.1	35.0
4.01 to 10.00	65.1	85.8	31.1
10.01+	65.4	81.5	42.4
All	**48.8**	**57.7**	**42.1**

Source: As above.

***Note*:** Incidence of indebtedness for farmers in different land holding classes does not vary but the agency for them varies radically. The poor farmers with small land holdings have limited access to institutional credit. They have to pay higher interest rate.

Table 15: Purposes for Credit

(Per cent)

Purposes	*1961*	*1971*	*1981*	*2002*
Productive	40.1	54.0	71.8	62.8
Unproductive	60.0	46.0	28.02	38.1

Source: As above.

***Note*:** Progressively the use of credit for business purposes as percentage to total credit borrowed has been increasing. In the near decade pressure on borrowing for consumption has been once again increasing. The reason could be reduced opportunities for productive investment as the results of research reaching the farming has been declining.

Table 16: Marketable Surplus

Crop	*Ratio*
Rice	43.0
Wheat	51.5
Coarse Cereals	43.1
Pulses	72.4
Oil seeds	79.6
Ground nut	68.3
Mustard and Rape	84.3
Other oil seeds	86.3
Sugar Cane	93.3
Cotton	100.0
Vegetables	83.0
Fruit	97.0

Source: 10th Five Year Plan Guru Committee.T.5.1.26.

Note: Before World War II the marketable surplus was close to 20-35% Compared to that the recent data suggest good deal of marketization of cereals. This suggests transition to modernization of agriculture. Non-food crops are mainly market crop including even vegetables and fruits.

Table 17: Urban and Rural Poverty Ratio

Year	*Rural*	*Urban*	*Total*
1973-74	56.4	49.9	54.9
1977-78	53.1	45.2	51.3
1983	45.6	40.8	44.5
1987-88	39.1	38.2	39.9
1993-94	37.3	32.4	31.0
1999-2000	27.1	23.6	26.1

Source: Planning Commission Estimates.

Note: poverty ratio has declined in rural and urban areas.
The decline has been sharp in urban area. This can be attributed to rapid growth in urban areas compared to that in rural areas.

Table 18: Population and Workforce Growth Employment Unemployment

Numbers Millions
Growth: Percentage

Items	*1983*	*1993-94*	*1999-2000*	*1983-4 to 1993-94*	*1993-94 to 1999-2000*
Total					
Population	718.20	894.21	1003.07	2.00	1.95
Labour Force	261.33	335.97	363.33	2.43	1.33
Work Force	230.57	315.84	336.95	2.70	1.07
Unemployment %	8.3	5.99	7.32	·	
Unemployed person days	21.76	20.13	26.58	-0.08	4.74
Rural					
Population	546.61	658.93	727.50	1.79	0.96
Labour Force	204.18	255.38	270.36	1.15	0.67
Work Force	187.92	241.04	250.89	2.40	
Unemployment %	7.96	5.61	7.21		
Unemployed person days	16.26	14.34	19.50	-1.19	5.26

(Contd.)

(Contd. Table 18)

Items	*1983*	*1993-94*	*1999-2000*	*1983-4 to 1993-94*	*1993-94 to 1999-2000*
Urban					
Population	171.59	234.98	276.47	3.04	2.40
Labor Force	57.15	80.60	92.95	3.33	2.40
Work Force	51.64	74.80	85.84	3.59	2.32
Unemployment %	4.54	7.19	7.65		
Unemployed person days	5.51	5.80	7.15	0.49	3.45

Source: 10th Five Year Plan T 5.1.

Data drawn from reports by NSSO and Population Censuses.

***Note*:** Population Growth is on decline Along with it the growth of Labour Force and Work force growth rate too declined.

Table 19 : Food Consumption Ratio Rural/Urban

Year	*Ratio*
1973-74	0.63
1993-94	0.61
2004-05	0.58

Source: NSS Surveys.

Note **: The decline though marginal is an indicator of underlying crisis. Food consumption does not expand in urban areas rapidly for the demand elasticity would decline with increase in incomes. Normally the food consumption in rural areas should gradually catch up with increasing incomes.**

Table 20: Growth Rate of Employment in Agriculture

From 1993-94—2004-05

Category	*1993-94—2004-5*
Agricultural Self-employment	1.01
Agricultural Wage Employment	-0.89
Total Agricultural Employment	0.40
Agricultural GIP	2.31
Implied employment elasticity	0.19
Real Agricultural Wage Growth	2.15

Note**:** Agriculture suffered from loss of wage employment. Self employment increased but at nearly half the rate of growth of agriculture. Wage rate kept pace with growth of agriculture. Implication of these developments could be The poor have less opportunity to benefit from growth of agriculture for employment lags behind. Those in employment may benefit from wage rise.

Rising wages with lack of employment may widen the hiatus of unemployment. Agriculture seems to substitute self employment for wage employment in the effort to save cost and increase personal incomes.

Table 21: Non-agricultural Employment Growth

From 1993-94—2004-05

Categories	*Growth Rate*
Non-agricultural Self-employment	3.81
Non-agricultural wage employment	3.18
Rural non-agricultural employment	3.52
Urban non-agricultural employment	3.46
Secondary Sector employment Growth rate	3.70
Tertiary sector employment growth rate	3.35
Total non-agricultural growth rate	3.29
Non- agricultural growth rate	7.71
Implied non-agricultural elasticity	0.45

Note : Employment growth rate in all sectors of non agricultural employment moved nearly in step. This is expected as incomes rise in secondary and tertiary Sectors benefit comparably during the transition stage. Besides non-agricultural sectors grew more rapidly in terms of their GDP. Thus, transition is less painful for non-agricultural sectors.

Bibliography

Bagchi, Amiya Kumar, Panchanan Das, Sadhan Kumar Chatopadhyay, Growth and Structural Change in the Economy of Gujarat 1970 – 2000, (2005) *Economic and Political Weekly* July 9 2005, pp. 3039 – 3047.

Barker Randolph, Robert W. Hert, Beth Rose (1985) 'The Rice Economy of Asia' Wasington D.C. 'Research for Future' 1985.

Dandekar V.M. and Rath Nilkanth. 'Poverty in India', Indian School of Political Economy. Bombay 1971.

Dandekar, V.M: "On Measurement of Poverty", *Economic and Political Weekly*, 16 : 30 (25 July, 1981) pp. 124-50. 67.

Dantwala M.L., (1937) Marketing of Raw Cotton in India. Longmans, Green.

Dantwala, M.L., Harsh Sethi and Pravin Visaria. 'Social Change through Voluntary Action'.

Dantwala, M.L., Indian Agricultural Development Since Independence.

Deb, Surgit:, 'Terms of Trade in Multi-Sectoral Framework': Analysis of All India and States Working Paper 112, Center for Development Economics, Department of Economics, Delhi School of Economics University of Delhi.

Hayami, Yugiro and Others: The Political Economy of Agricultural Production, (Sydney, London, Boston) Allen and Unwin 1986.

Hirschman, Albert D., Generalised Linkage Approach to Development, with Special Reference to Staples, In Manning Nash (ed) 'Essays in Economic Development and Cultural Change, Chicago, Chicago University Press 1977, pp. 67-98.

Mosse, David, Sanjeev Gupta, Vidya Shah:, 'On the Margins in a City: Adivasi Seasonal Labor in Western India'.

Mungekar B.L. (1992), Political Economics of Terms of Trade, Himalayan Publishing House Mumbai.

Okhava, Kazushi and Bruce F. Johnson: (1969) 'The Transferability of the Japanese Pattern of Modernizing Traditional Agriculture, pages 277 to 310 In 'The Role of Agriculture in Economic Development, by 'Eric Thorbecke', National Bureau of Economic Research New York.

Pandit, V.N., Harish Mani, G. Balchandran, C.H. Shah (2010), Technological Change and Factor Substitution In Indian Agriculture, in Current Issues in Indian Agriculture (Ed) Jagannath Lenke, Serial Publishers, Delhi.

Rao V.M. and D.V. Gopalappan (2004) 'Agricultural Growth and Farmer Distress', Institute for Social and Economic Change, Bangalore.

Rath, Nilakanth (1985) 'Prices, Costs of Production and Terms of Trade of Indian Agriculture', Indian Journal of Agricultural Economics (49) 4.

Schultz, Theodore William, (1945) Agriculture in an Unstable Economy New York, McGraw Hill.

Schultz, Theodore William, (1964) 'Transforming Traditional Agriculture' Yale University Press, New Haven.

Schultz, Theodore William (1981) Investing in People, Berkeley and Los Angeles, University of California Press.

Schultz, Theodore William (1993) The Economics of Being Poor, Cambridge, Massachusetts, Blackwell Publishers.

Shah C. H. and Vimal Shah, Sudarshan Iyengar, Agricultural Growth and Equity: A Micro-Level Experience, pp. 1991 - 235.

Shah, C.H.: The Demand For Higher-Status Food and Nutrition in Rural India: The Experience of Matar Taluka. Regression Analyses.

Shah, C.H. (1957) Problem of Small Farmers in India, Vora and Co. Bombay.

Shukla, Tara: (1965) Capital Formation in Indian Agriculture, Vora and Company.

Siva Subramanian, S. (2000), The National Income of India.

Timmer, C. Peter, (1987) 'Crop Diversification in Rice Based Agriculture, Conceptual and Policy Issues' Washington, World Bank.

Timmer, C. Peter, Walter T. Falcon and Scott R. Pearson, 'Food Policy Analysis, John Hopkins University Press for the World Bank.

Index

Z